COURSE CREATION

SIMPLIFIED

THE 6-PHASE SYSTEM TO PROFITABLE
ONLINE COURSES

JIMMY NARAINE

TABLE OF CONTENTS

INTRODUCTION

THIS BOOK WILL CHANGE YOUR LIFE IF YOU LET IT

Welcome to *Course Creation Simplified*! I've never met you, but let me make a guess about why you're here. You opened this book because there's a fire in your belly. You're an expert in what you do and you've been dabbling in the idea of producing an online course.

You may already be writing blog posts, creating social media content... maybe even sharing your message in front of a live audience. However, for some reason, the thought of creating and posting instructional videos online makes you panic. Sometimes, in those rare moments of inspiration, you tune into that quiet yet encouraging voice whispering deep inside: "You can do it." But sadly, every time you ponder getting started, resistance slaps you in the face. Back to square one!

Perhaps you're afraid of not being good enough. "Building a full-blown course? I can barely get myself to make a short YouTube video. Why would anyone care about what I have to say anyway?"

Maybe you are trapped in the paradox of choice. It seems there are hundreds of paths you could take. You can't choose which one to take so procrastination ends up winning every time.

Or perhaps you've already tried to take the first steps, but you're overwhelmed by the sheer size of the task. You're confused by the technology. You don't even know if your process makes any sense. You worry you won't get a return on your investment. Once again, you become paralyzed by the unknowns.

If you can relate to any of these (mental) roadblocks, then welcome, you've come to the right place. You are not alone. At this very moment, millions of people just like you are trying to figure out how to share their knowledge with the world. Sadly, most of them will never begin. And many who do begin will never see the project through to completion.

The good news is that the process for creating an online course does NOT need to be overwhelming. I'm living proof that anyone can do this, and there are so many others like me.

If someone had told me a decade ago, when I was broke and heartbroken, that I would have a global impact one day, I wouldn't have believed them. Fast forward, and over the years I've explored almost 100 countries while teaching half a million people across the world—all from daring to build one online course (and then consistently growing from there). Make no mistake. The journey has been challenging. I started from absolute zero, and at some point I almost gave up. Almost gave up. It is so sad to even write that as I'm fully aware that there are people out there just like me, who are meant to create, but threw in the towel before really getting started. Along the way I've learned that anything is possible when you have a solid action plan and take daily steps toward your goals.

People from many different walks of life successfully publish courses each and every day in spite of their initial resistance, confusion, and fear. Like me, most have learned that something that first felt overwhelming is, in fact, achievable. You just have to make a decision that building an online course is important to you. Then, you have to commit to seeing it through and *follow the proven process* I am giving you in this book.

Course Creation Simplified is the simple yet powerful blueprint I wish I'd had when I was getting started. In the following chapters, I'll share a proven methodology that has worked not only for me but for thousands of other experts who have also started from scratch. At this point, I'm tempted to share various case studies to prove how valuable my process is, but I don't want to turn this book into a typical "look at me! I helped all those people" self-indulgent pep talk. Instead, throughout the book, I will share with you only the most relevant and empowering stories while focusing on actionable steps. I intend to cut out all the unnecessary fluff. However, if you're curious about the success of people I've helped, you can visit **www.jimmynaraine.com/testimonials** to learn about the people who have used my teachings to upgrade their lives.

WHAT YOU WILL LEARN IN THIS BOOK

My intention is to guide you through a comprehensive yet straightforward action plan that will guide you as you build your first online course. I will show you that something seemingly complicated can be simple when you follow the right blueprint. Most importantly, you will gain the confidence necessary to get your course out there as soon as possible.

I'm not going to bury you with hundreds of flashy tactics you would probably never use. I also don't want you to overthink what it takes to become an international bestseller or to rack up thousands of five-star reviews. In the words of billionaire entrepreneur Peter Thiel, it's about getting you "from 0 to 1." I'll do that by teaching you evergreen principles and systems. After all, if you don't release your first course, none of the flashy stuff matters.

In this book I break everything down into seven major clusters which are divided into chapters to make the learning process powerful, yet easy to follow. We will start by addressing course creation fundamentals, understanding the big picture, and upgrading your mindset. However, we will quickly move into specific processes with explanations, clear action steps, and exercises.

In **Part 1: Become a Creator: Why YOU and Why Now?** we will discuss everything you need to know before embarking on your course creation journey. I'll explain why our global transition into a "personal transformation" economy is good news for an expert like you, and why now is the best time to publish.

In **Part 2: Your Niche & Audience Identification Phase,** you will learn how to make an educated decision about what to teach and how to find your ideal audience. No matter where you are on the "course creation paralysis" spectrum—from feeling trapped in the paradox of choice to doubting that there is anything you could teach—my process will give you the confidence and clarity you'll need to swiftly move forward.

Part 3: Blueprint for Creating World-Class Content, is all about designing your entire course roadmap, from building an intelligent course structure to designing a curriculum. You will also learn how to create captivating content that people want to consume and are willing to pay for. Here, I'll teach you powerful A to Z strategies that will help you WOW your target audience.

In **Part 4: Produce Top-Quality Courses on Any Budget,** I'll show you how you can produce your course on any budget (or no budget at all). Some of my strategies may shock you. You will also learn how to deliver your material with confidence and charisma. For many people, just the mere thought of standing in front of a camera can be a dreadful experience. It doesn't have to be like that, and I will show you exactly how to overcome those insecurities and find your voice.

In **Part 5: Publishing and Marketing for Impact and Profit,** we'll delve into publishing and marketing. Many people have the erroneous belief that "If you just build it, they will come." In truth, if you want to attain real success it's up to you to attract your viewers. For that reason, it's vital to understand your publishing and marketing options and to choose the optimal strategy based on your specific circumstances, needs, and objectives. I don't want you to get lost in the sea of possible scenarios, so I will break everything down to make it easy for you to decide what works best for you.

In **Part 6: Harness Your Fear and Develop True Confidence,** we'll work on overcoming your fears and building the true confidence necessary to successfully teach online. You'll learn real-life tools and mindset shifts that will radically change how you perceive—and banish—fear. If you bought this book solely to learn about the course creation process and don't lack anything in the confidence department, feel free to skip this part. However, based on my experience, even the most confident individuals struggle with occasional self-doubts, so I recommend that you at least skim through this section so you don't miss any key takeaways.

Finally, **Part 7: Taking that Leap,** will serve as the final push to get you started. Here, we will tie together everything you've learned. I want to make sure that nothing stops you from embarking on this exciting journey of building your online course empire.

In addition, I've created a **completely free online page with links to all the resources** I mention in this book. There, I'll post tools, case studies, checklists, or any other resource that I mention in the book. With an electronic resource I can make sure that everything I share with you stays up to date (including links). You can find the resources page here: **www.jimmynaraine.com/ coursecreationresources**

WHAT YOU WON'T FIND IN THIS BOOK

I'm aware that some business books continuously mention high-ticket programs in the hopes of converting readers into paying customers. As you will soon discover, you won't find that in *Course Creation Simplified*. In fact, as you read these pages you will notice that I never aggressively pitch anything. My business is what makes my living, and this book is on my "positive global impact" bucket list. Everything else is just the cherry on top!

Also, you've probably noticed that many people teaching how to make money online get the bulk of their revenue from teaching others how to make money; they don't "walk the walk." That is not my cup of tea. I've spent almost a decade teaching personal and professional development through affordable online courses, corporate training, and live events. I've only started sharing my course creation methodology recently because my audience keeps asking me to share. It got to the point where even after I gave a presentation on an unrelated subject, people would still come up and ask me about course creation. Eventually, I realized that I had no choice but to block a good one-thousand hours in my calendar, fight resistance, slay some internal dragons, and deliver this book to my audience.

In **Course Creation Simplified** I'm not going to promise you $100,000 or $1,000,000 with the launch of an online course. It's not about teaching you how to create and desperately push overpriced products, while you rationalize the price by thinking that "otherwise, people won't see the value." It's also not about showing you how to cut corners and make money selling huge amounts of subpar content.

This book is about opening the doors to new possibilities, proving to you that online course creation doesn't have to be scary or confusing. Will you make a huge amount of money offering your unique expertise to the world? It's possible, and I genuinely hope you will. However, this book is about much more than that.

BUILDING A STRONG FOUNDATION

Every person is in a slightly different situation, and the subject of building an online course can be vast. Entire books could be written about content creation, branding, or marketing alone. For that reason, in **Course Creation Simplified** I will not attempt to answer the thousands of technical questions and explore the hundreds of possible scenarios that are out there. I will do my best to steer clear from any unnecessary and distracting rabbit holes.

Instead, I will give you the fundamental knowledge necessary for you to successfully publish your *first* online course. I will help you build a strong foundation so you'll fully understand how the course creation process works. Most importantly, I will guide you every step along the way without triggering that feeling of overwhelm.

In case you're wondering, I've tried various platforms, from co-creating a membership site to authoring a QUEST with Mindvalley, but I publish most of my content on Udemy. Don't worry about a platform at the moment. You will benefit tremendously from the content of this book no matter which course platform you choose. In Part 5, I'll discuss various publishing options and explore the pros and cons of each. Until then, open your mind, explore this guide one page at a time, and soon enough, the seemingly complex issues will become simple.

WHY SHOULD YOU EVEN LISTEN TO ME?

I know that somewhere in the back of your mind you may be wondering, "It all sounds exciting, but who is Jimmy Naraine, and why should I listen to him?" Well, I certainly do not claim to know everything. I always strive to maintain the "white belt" mentality and keep my ego in check. However, selling over half a million courses has taught me a thing or two. I got into this business 10 years ago (after realizing that climbing the corporate ranks wasn't my calling) when very few people were producing online courses. Back then, there were almost no resources available. I've made all the mistakes and learned many hard lessons. My goal is to make this book the ultimate evergreen beginner's manual for aspiring course creators, like a GPS that won't lead you down a dead-end road. So, while this book is all about YOU (not me), let me tell you a little bit about why I'm qualified to teach this topic.

On my journey, I've befriended, helped, worked with, and shared the stage with some immensely successful people. I've also helped thousands of individuals turn their expertise into online courses, including some of my friends and family members. One of them is my father. Several years ago, I convinced (or more like brow-beat) him to finally share his knowledge with the digital world. After long months of reluctance, he eventually gave in and followed my blueprint (the very same one provided in this book) to create his first virtual course. Fast forward, and he is currently teaching more than 150,000 people online. Naturally, you may be curious to know who my father is. If that's the case, google Dr. Roy Naraine or find his courses on Udemy: **www.udemy.com/user/ roynaraine/** (We look nothing alike, do we?) As a fun fact, in late 2022 my mom broke out of her comfort zone, learned videography, and joined my father on the content creation journey. Their experience is a testament to a simple truth that your age should never be a barrier and it's never too late to get started.

To date, I've created more than 40 online courses that have received more than 70,000 certified top ratings. Many of my courses have been recommended in *Forbes*, *Entrepreneur*, and *Business Insider*. I also co-authored Course Pro with Mindvalley's founder Vishen Lakhiani, which has been one of Mindvalley's best-selling products. I've taught course creation at countless international events such as Mindvalley, Digital|K, DesignHill, and Nomad Cruise. Finally, here's what Oscar-winning producer, James Skotchdopole (*Django*, *The Reverent*, *Birdman*) says about **Course Creation Simplified**:

> *"Jimmy Naraine is a master at breaking apart the difficult and complex. With the most simple and basic steps, he plainly demonstrates how to digest each and every morsel of information, and make an actionable plan. Jimmy Naraine is a true teaching savant."*

I grew up in post-communist Poland. I had anxiety and confidence issues, no money, no mentors, and didn't speak English. If someone told me back in my youth that one day I'd teach people from almost every country on the planet, I wouldn't have believed them. I do know that my journey stands as living proof that building world-class online courses is not an innate talent. It's a skill anybody (including you) can learn.

You have a course in you. The fact that you're holding this book in your hands suggests that you're already burning to share your knowledge with others. Imagine the positive impact your content will have on your students, some of whom will share what they learn from you, passing the knowledge forward and adding to the ripple effect across time and space.

We can't predict the size of the dent you'll make in the universe. But one thing is for certain. If you don't get started, you'll never know.

I encourage you to trust the process, take action, and treat course creation not as a chore, but an exciting adventure. In no time, we will get you to proudly release your first course.

Let's go!

- **Jimmy**

PART 1

BECOME A CREATOR: WHY YOU AND WHY NOW?

THE BLESSING OF AUTOMATED IMPACT (AND INCOME)

Here's an excerpt from my journal in April 2020:

"The sound of the ambulance is getting louder. It's the ninth time I've heard the siren today, and I'm just hoping that whoever is inside will get help on time. We are in the middle of the Covid-19 lockdown in Germany and I'm shocked how quickly the reality we all had been taking for granted has shifted. The new "normal" feels a bit like a bad dream, but the implications are real. Countless

people are not only getting physically sick, but also losing jobs, seeing their businesses tank, and experiencing the mental anguish resulting from uncertainty and social isolation. Even though I fully appreciate the gravity of the situation and feel tremendous compassion for everyone affected, I can't help but experience another emotion: GRATITUDE."

I felt gratitude because my family members and friends were safe, but there was more to it. I was also thankful for not losing my ability to impact people all over the world. Even though my speaking engagements and some planned adventures had been canceled, it was a blessing to know that my content would keep making a positive impact. In the middle of the "COVID winter" I knew that no matter how long the lockdown would last, I could continue to support my online community.

That feeling of contribution is priceless; however, to be completely frank, it's not just about making an impact today as a guide, a teacher. I know that as long as the internet exists I'll be able to generate a recurring income. An income that allows me to live life on my terms and to support the people and causes I care about most. It's a miracle to be able to share ideas, thoughts, knowledge, and experiences with people in all corners of the world, and make a solid income in the process—all with just a few clicks of a mouse.

CHAPTER 1

FUNDAMENTAL MINDSET SHIFT

WAITING FOR THE GREEN LIGHT

People often ask me: "So, Jimmy, when is the best time to publish a course?"

My answer is always the same. "Just do it. Do it now."

Naturally, I don't mean that you should drop everything else and rush through the process for the sake of "shipping" your half-baked product next Friday. What I mean is that we often squander opportunities by waiting way too long for the green light, not realizing that realistically, that GO signal may never come. You read that correctly. For most of us, the light will always remain yellow. This is why it's essential to commit (ideally publicly) to a deadline and kick-start the process in spite of any excuses or emotional discomfort standing in your way.

The truth is that no matter how knowledgeable and experienced you are in what you can teach, you will never feel completely ready to create an online course. But there's a big difference between FEELING ready and BEING ready. Even though I've published more than 40 courses, I still experience moments of self-doubt. That's when I remember that real courage is not about being fearless. On the contrary, it's about acknowledging your fears and stepping into the arena anyway.

When you start producing content you will also start learning and gaining new insights. Naturally, you will have a temptation to implement all your new ideas immediately. However, this approach will keep you stuck in the perpetual draft mode. The mindset of "this has to be perfect" will mean you will never complete your work, much less share it. Even though your content might be phenomenal, nobody will ever get to experience it until you dare to take the leap.

Instead of waiting for perfection (which will never come, by the way), you need to commit to a firm date and release the best version of a course you are capable of at that time. You will never feel completely ready, but it doesn't mean that you aren't. Just do it. Keep in mind that you are not printing a fixed product that cannot be changed. On the contrary, all leading online course platforms make it almost effortless for you to upgrade your courses in real time. Being mindful that whatever you create in digital form does not have to be set in stone will help you to overcome any toxic perfectionism. What's more, remember that as you keep gaining more knowledge and experience, you can always publish new online courses.

Having said that, I do understand that it is scary to share your baby with the world. You can probably paint various worst case scenarios in your mind, convinced that at least some of them will happen. Just know that these fears are just illusions. Follow my system and you can prevent them from happening and you can easily fix something that does go wrong.

THINGS TO REMEMBER

- Stop waiting for the perfect moment, commit to a deadline, and take action now.

- Avoid getting stuck in the perpetual draft mode. Remember that after releasing a course, you can keep improving it.

- Use my proven system to overcome potential challenges and confidently share your work.

CHAPTER 2

PROVEN SOLUTIONS TO YOUR TEN MOST COMMON FEARS

Let's address the most likely fears you may have about creating an online course and explore proven solutions to them.

FEAR #1: I AM NOT GOOD ENOUGH.

Solution: You don't need to be the most prominent expert in the world. You just need to know more than your target audience, have a real passion for your subject, and be relatable. You also need to do something most people will never get themselves to do—follow the process and publish. (If the issue goes deeper and you struggle with self-esteem issues, we'll discuss that challenge later in Part 6.)

FEAR #2: I'M SUCCESSFUL IN MY FIELD, BUT I'M AFRAID THE COURSE WILL NOT LIVE UP TO EVERYONE'S EXPECTATIONS.

Solution: I feel you. I too have been a victim of this fear. For instance, I experienced it when I was invited to speak before a big audience for the first time. I was afraid that my performance wouldn't live up to my brand image. I feared being outed as an imposter.

Eventually, I broke that spell. Here's something that helps me. Instead of being paralyzed by the immense pressure to perform, I openly admit to my audience that I do not know everything but that I'll do my absolute best to help them. In many of the introductions to my courses I admit that even though I'm an expert, I don't have all the answers and the more I learn, the more I realize how much more there is to learn. Your viewers will be already aware of all the things you've accomplished (more about that later in the book). So counter that by showing authentic humility. A mixture of vulnerability and credibility is always a winning combination that will captivate your audience.

FEAR #3: WHAT IF NOBODY BUYS MY COURSE? I'LL LOOK LIKE A FAILURE.

Solution: First of all, nobody needs to know how many courses you've sold. If you host the course on your own platform, nobody can see your stats. If you host it in a marketplace such as Udemy, there are clever ways to create initial credibility. For instance, you can give free access to your inner circle to boost your stats right from the beginning. (We'll discuss that strategy in the marketing section.)

Second, when it comes down to it, people are too busy worrying about their own challenges to care about yours. You reading my book is a good example. Do you know how many copies I've sold so far? Have you looked into my profile and comprehensively analyzed my best and worst-performing courses? Probably not. The point I'm trying to make is simple. People don't care as much as you think, so go ahead, be bold, do your best, and let the rest follow.

FEAR #4: PEOPLE WILL NOT LIKE MY CONTENT

Solution: There are two things I need to address. If some people don't resonate with something, their attention ends up flowing elsewhere. Nobody wants to waste their time on something they don't like in a world with millions of options. In other words, if your content doesn't resonate with someone they will simply move on.

As well, and this may sound counterintuitive, but some people not liking your content is a good thing. No matter what you do and how well you do it, you will never make everyone happy. This is why you should never aim to please everyone in the first place. Instead, create your niche (more about that soon), produce what you believe in, and find the courage to focus your course to serve a very specific audience. Instead of going broad to try to catch people who may not resonate with your course, focus on the exact people who absolutely love (and need) what you create. It is one of the most empowering mindset shifts you could ever experience, and it will set you free.

This reminds me of a funny anecdote David Sedaris shared in his online masterclass. He humbly admitted that there is nothing special about him and that he still can't believe he's even allowed to speak on the radio due to his peculiar voice. David admitted that a teacher once told him that after having students listen to one of his audiobooks, one of the kids commented: "I just feel sorry for that old lady." The teacher asked, "What old lady?" The kid exclaimed, "The one they hired to read that stupid book!"

Wondering who David Sedaris is? He is a writer who has sold more than 12 million books.

FEAR #5: WHAT IF I GET TERRIBLE REVIEWS?

Solution: Focus all your energy on creating a value-packed course that will generate plenty of excellent reviews. If you do that, an occasional one-star rating won't make any difference. The good news is that all of this is under your control, and frankly, this is an excellent example of a situation in which fear can be useful. The concern about receiving negative reviews can either paralyze you OR push you to go above and beyond. Whenever you receive constructive criticism, you can use it to upgrade your course in real time. Besides, I've got your back. If you implement the advice and strategies in this book, you won't have to worry about terrible ratings and the occasional bad comment will get lost in the sea of genuine praise.

FEAR #6: EVERYTHING ON THIS TOPIC HAS ALREADY BEEN COVERED

Solution: This is never true. Here's why. Remember, it's never about the information itself, but about how you package it while adding your unique flavor. Different individuals resonate with different teachers. Everyone is wired differently, which, combined with distinct life experiences, mindset, and preferences, impacts their choices. There is not just one right way of teaching something.

For example, I'm fascinated by the topic of leadership. I especially enjoy books written by Jocko Willink and Leif Babin, as I find their approaches, stories, and interpretations immensely valuable. Their leadership content is comprehensive, but does it mean that I will not consume any other resources on this topic? Of course not. I always try my hardest to expand my horizons. Even though the core leadership concepts discussed in various publications may be the same, I'm always curious to learn about them from different angles.

When you build your course don't be deterred if others may have already tackled the same subject. Focus on injecting your personal "flavor" in terms of unique delivery, authentic personality, storytelling, choice of examples, and case studies. Instead of trying to please everyone, focus on being yourself and on giving specific value to your target audience.

FEAR #7: THE PROCESS IS TOO COMPLICATED, AND I'M AFRAID I WILL GET LOST

Solution: You are holding the solution to this fear in your hands. As I mentioned, the process doesn't have to be confusing when you have the right guidance. As humans, we are hardwired to fear the unknown. Stick around. It's going to be okay.

FEAR #8: I'M NOT A TECHNICAL PERSON. I DON'T KNOW ANYTHING ABOUT FILMING, EDITING, AND PUBLISHING.

Solution: You don't need to be a tech wizard! Truth be told, today's technology makes it extremely easy, affordable, and intuitive to build your classes. In terms of publishing, the good news is that established platforms such as Udemy, Thinkific, Teachable, and Kajabi make course creation very simple. After my persistent nudging, my brother and father (who had zero tech experience) released a bestselling course filmed with an iPhone 4. Stick with me, and we'll walk through the process step by step. You've got this!

FEAR #9: THE CAMERA DOESN'T LIKE ME! I WILL LOOK WEIRD.

Solution: Think about your favorite teachers. My guess is that most of them weren't supermodels. In fact, since we connect with others through our common humanity, we are more likely to form bonds with those who remind us of our imperfect selves. Forget about your looks; nobody cares. People like to learn from instructors they can trust and resonate with. It's more about your passion for teaching, presentation skills (which is a skill you can and will learn), and unique set of experiences than the way you look.

FEAR #10: I'M NOT A GREAT PRESENTER

Solution: Most exceptional presenters are not born, but made. For each example of a "naturally born" speaker, I can pull out ten cases of those who were not naturally gifted but got to the top through sheer perseverance. If you feel like your presentation skills are lacking, no worries. In Part 5 we'll discuss how you can improve your delivery. Plus, I'll grant you free access to my videos about confident video presenting. No strings attached.

USE FEAR AS LEVERAGE

I hope that by now you see that your fears about creating a course are just barriers you've thrown up in your mind. Having said that, there is one fear you should magnify and utilize to constantly fuel massive action. That is the fear of ending up living your life with the pain of regret, the regret of actions you didn't take and a gnawing awareness that you squandered your true potential.

Are you learning from this book so far? Well, let me tell you, it almost didn't happen. When I was a university student, I discovered the Bible. The Bible of Digital Nomads that is, written by Tim Ferriss. His book *The 4-hour Workweek* served as a catalyst that opened my mind to the fact that I could build a location-independent business while exploring the world. It showed me what was possible and propelled me to shape a new reality for myself. Sometimes I wonder where I would be now if Tim Ferriss hadn't found the courage to publish his work. It is completely possible that without that trigger I wouldn't be doing what I'm doing, and… you wouldn't be reading my book now (The ripple effect at work…).

YOUR ACTION STEP

I want you to think about books, articles, courses, movies, podcasts, and speeches that have influenced or formed your life. Jot them down on a piece of paper or in the margins of this book. Then ask yourself: "How would my life be different if that particular work had never been created? How much would I be missing out on in my life if the author of that piece of content hadn't summoned the courage to not only create it but then go on to share it with the world?" It is profound to consider, isn't it?

As a shy teenager living in a small Polish town, I had many limiting beliefs. Discovering the works of Tony Robbins, Brian Tracy, and Dale Carnegie opened the doors to new possibilities. Through their books I realized that I had the power to bend reality to my will and consciously custom-create my future. I began to obsess over self-improvement, learning English, and studying for my final exams. I was able to bootstrap myself to a British university, eventually landing a job at Goldman Sachs, only to realize I was living someone else's dream. However, those experiences were instrumental in building the confidence to leave the corporate world in my rear-view mirror and dive deep into the world of entrepreneurship. Sometimes, I wonder what would've happened to me if my early mentors hadn't found the courage and perseverance to publish their books.

YOUR GLOBAL IMPACT

By sharing your message you could have just as significant an impact on your audience as those writers had on me. If you don't share the knowledge you have in you, you are not only holding yourself back. You are also doing a disservice to everyone who could be positively impacted by your content. If you don't publish your course you're depriving your potential students of the opportunity to improve their lives and create a ripple effect for others to benefit from. Today, I encourage you to be bold and remember that sharing your message is more than just some personal goal. It's your calling. Your responsibility.

THINGS TO REMEMBER

- Avoid the trap of the perpetual "yellow" light. The best time to build a course is now.
- Not feeling ready has nothing to do with being ready.
- Let go of fear disguised as perfectionism and commit to a firm date.
- Most of the worst-case scenarios you can paint in your mind can be prevented or easily fixed.
- When you don't share your gift with the world, you do a disservice to everyone who could benefit from it.

CHAPTER 3

THE "PERSONAL TRANSFORMATION" ECONOMY IS YOUR OPPORTUNITY

OUR REALITY IS MOVING ONLINE

Our global culture is making an exponential shift to the "online economy." For example, some of my friends (including my girlfriend) had been running very successful event and fitness businesses. Then COVID-19 happened, and those who didn't have a Plan B found themselves under extreme financial pressure due to lockdowns and event cancellations. Sadly, some of those businesses barely survived and their future still feels very uncertain, to say the least.

Perhaps you faced a similar predicament. I know experts in various fields who were making all of their income from in-person client work. Amid the crisis, they tried to adapt and move their operations online. However, it's challenging. For most of them, the internet was completely uncharted territory. To make matters worse, many people don't fully understand the concept of scaling. In essence, they're trapped in the paradigm of exchanging their time for money.

THE DEATH OF THE INFORMATION AGE AND THE RISE OF THE "PERSONAL TRANSFORMATION" ECONOMY

Many people believe that we're still in the information economy. I strongly disagree. Nowadays, information is not only cheap. In many cases, it's totally free. The overflow of data can be overwhelming; we are bombarded by thousands of stimuli every day. The paradox of choice is no longer something that only a few experience. It's one of the most prevalent phenomena of our time. We all consume tremendous amounts of information. However, the question is: How do you distinguish what's truly valuable from just minutia? It's tricky, and this is precisely why people no longer value pure information. What they really care about is clear *guidance* from sources they can trust.

Consider this. Why do hundreds of millions of people pay for online courses and books even though a lot of the same information is freely available? The reason is simple. People crave clarity that comes from following proven processes designed by trustworthy experts.

For example, if Sally wants to build her first website on a tiny budget, which option sounds more compelling?

A: Going through countless YouTube videos trying to figure out which ones are legit and in what order to watch them.

B: Spending $20 on a step-by-step course that has plenty of verified five-star ratings, which was designed by an expert, backed with a money-back guarantee and an interactive Q/A section.

Let's use Sally's example to consider the hidden cost in terms of time and effort of trying to "design" your learning plan using only free resources. Finding the right resources can be confusing and tedious. On top of that, there's a real risk of consuming poor quality, perhaps even misleading, content. Then it may be difficult to determine how to connect different learning pieces to see the website creation process through to completion. All things considered, it's often much better to invest a little money in order to gain clarity, learn from a proven process, and most importantly, reclaim countless hours of otherwise wasted time.

REDEFINING THE MEANING OF "EXPERT"

People want to learn from the best in the world, right? Not necessarily. In fact, in most cases, they don't. Reading this, you may be thinking: "Come on, Jimmy. This doesn't make much sense." Frankly, even though the above statement may sound unlikely, it is true.

Here's a great example. On Masterclass.com, it costs $180 to get 12-month access to almost 200 video courses created by celebrities such as Martin Scorsese, Samuel L. Jackson, Jodie Foster, Neil deGrasse Tyson, Malcolm Gladwell, Dan Brown, and Carlos Santana. It sounds like a no-brainer, doesn't it? After all, nobody can compete with the big shots, correct? Not exactly.

It's counterintuitive, but it's just not how the world of online courses works, and I'll explain why. Since 2010, more than 57 million people have chosen to collectively spend billions of dollars buying Udemy courses. Other online course hosts, such as Kajabi, Thinkific, Teachable, and Skillshare, also generate enormous revenue. What all those platforms have in common is that as long as you fulfill the minimum quality requirements, they will allow you to become an instructor. No questions asked and certainly no need to be famous.

I want you to ponder a simple yet profound question: Why would millions of people eagerly give their money to instructors who they don't know? What makes them prioritize that option, especially considering such easy access to celebrity teachers on Masterclass.com? It looks like something doesn't add up here!

The answer may surprise you. Being a world-class expert is no longer enough. There is an ingredient that is proving to be significantly more critical in today's world of education. I'm referring to **relatability**. People want to learn from those they trust, respect, and most importantly, can relate to.

Here's another thought experiment.

Which coach would you rather pick in order to help you accomplish your New Year's goal of losing 20 kilograms?

A) Jack, a competition-winning fitness model with exceptional genetics (merely inhaling the gym air makes him grow muscle), 25 years of professional experience, and no history of weight issues.

B) Trinity, a single mom who developed a passion for fitness while losing 40 kilograms in just three years, going from bedridden to regularly completing half marathons, and successfully helping others get fit.

I regularly ask this exact question when presenting to various audiences, and whether I'm in Tokyo, Buenos Aires, New York, or Berlin, the result is always the same. The majority admit that they would opt for classes with the single mom. The rationale is simple. People love to learn from those who have experienced the same pain and can relate to their situation. After all, successfully overcoming a massive challenge is living proof that the person has a solution that works.

If you struggle with weight issues, you know that Trinity is fully aware of the emotions you experience. Moreover, you are not afraid of her negative judgment. She understands you because she was once in your shoes. Jack may have more in-depth knowledge after decades of living and breathing fitness, but for most people, this is not as important as being able to relate to their teacher.

Naturally, everyone is different, and I'm aware that you may be thinking: "Well, I'd always choose a top trainer." As a life-long athlete myself, I can relate to that. However, after performing this thought experiment with thousands of people, it cannot be denied that the word "expert" doesn't mean what we often think it does. We have to redefine it in the context of contemporary education.

I know amazing individuals who have a lot of value to share with the world... but they're stuck. They're stuck in the idea that they are not good enough to teach online. They keep procrastinating and rationalizing to themselves that they still have too much to learn. They never feel truly ready to "pull the trigger." Their inner dialogue keeps whispering, "Well, if I push myself to get better, then I'll be ready to publish a course next year." Does this sound familiar?

This cycle can perpetuate itself, and you may wake up one day feeling the tremendous weight of regret. Give yourself the credit you deserve! Remember, it is not really about you. It is about serving the audience that needs to hear your unique voice.

WHAT ABOUT THE COMPETITION?

Most people perceive competition to be something they need to dwarf, to dominate. They believe that the online course arena is a zero-sum game, embracing the mindset of: "If you sell more courses, it means I sell less." That's not exactly true. When you focus on creating unique value, suddenly you become one-of-a-kind. While you shouldn't disregard your competition (I will touch on it later in the book), you also shouldn't overly preoccupy yourself with it. Instead, keep asking yourself: "How can I add my unique flavor and make my courses irresistible?"

In my early days I knew that I needed to stand out. After all, nobody had any idea who I was. Since I'd always loved traveling, I built a team of people who shared my dreams of world exploration. We decided to shoot our content in faraway places such as the Canary Islands, Vietnam, and Thailand, to name just a few. Naturally, you may wonder how it was possible to pay for the entire team to travel the world with me. The simple answer is, I didn't have to, but more about that in Part 5 of this book. The point I'm trying to make here is that, instead of reactively worrying about your competition, be proactive about leveraging your unique style to stand out from the crowd.

THINGS TO REMEMBER

- We are no longer in the information age but rather the "personal transformation" economy, where people value clear, customized guidance over pure information.

- Relatability is more important than being a world-class expert. People want to learn from those they trust, respect, and can resonate with.

- While it's foolish to completely disregard your competition, you shouldn't overly preoccupy yourself with it. Instead, focus on adding your unique value to make your courses irresistible.

- Standing out from the competition requires leveraging your unique style and finding innovative ways to attract an audience.

CHAPTER 4

BUILDING A COURSE WILL CHANGE YOUR LIFE

If you are 100% set on why exactly you need to build a course, and what benefits you are looking to get from doing so, you may feel tempted to skip this chapter. However, I encourage you to at least skim through the following pages, since it will help you further clarify your vision and you may discover a completely fresh angle.

I want to make sure that you not only embark on but also successfully complete the entire course creation journey. If you focus solely on all the work lying ahead of you, without first creating a compelling vision, you are likely to get into trouble. After the initial phase of being "fired up," you may begin to feel stressed and overwhelmed. Sound familiar? At some point we've all set out on some new project and lost steam after a while.

There's nothing wrong with enjoying a well-deserved rest, but it can be dangerous if not justified. Oftentimes, it's pure procrastination in disguise. As you know, sometimes "life just happens" and the next thing you know, you lose the momentum. In fact, I experienced it while editing this book! It's a debilitating feeling. I want you to be mentally ready for the long haul.

So how can you prevent procrastination from taking your dream to the grave? Instead of simply going through the motions, it's essential that you really sell yourself on the idea of building an online course. You must keep fueling your fire every step along the way. You can do this by clearly defining the tremendous benefits that becoming a course author will bring and by shifting your mindset from passive to "**default aggressive**." In other words, you have to become obsessed.

TURNING MOTIVATION INTO DRIVE

Taking the time to carefully define a compelling **"Why"** is crucial if you want to feel passionate about this project from start to finish. It's not just about a quick injection of motivation, though. It's not merely about positively changing your mental state, either. When you create an exciting vision for yourself, you will feel driven.

Creating a strong "Why" is about fundamentally shifting your perception of what releasing an online course means to you. It's about consciously deciding why your new mission is so important. Your irresistible "Why" will keep you fired up even when faced with unexpected challenges. Only then will you be able to create and take full advantage of golden opportunities that will inevitably appear along the way.

"Overnight success" is a myth. Sadly, we live in a culture of cutting corners and expecting massive results with minimum effort. In reality, any real success takes work, perseverance, and occasionally getting slapped in the face by unexpected predicaments.

> *Didn't get a six-pack in 3 weeks? Screw it. I quit.*

> *Didn't make $10,000 in the first month of running a business? Screw it. I quit.*

> *Have difficulty absorbing information? Screw learning. I quit.*

Strike a chord? We've all been there. But the truth is... anything that's worth pursuing requires effort, perseverance, and patience to see it through. If you really want something, you can't quit.

This is why knowing exactly what you want and *why* you want it is so important.

We all face self-doubts. We hesitate because we're unsure. We all have days when we don't feel like doing anything. This is why you need a strong anchor that will keep you on track. To define your "Why," you need to focus on the benefits your online course will bring you, and yes, that includes some of your "selfish" desires.

I still remember publishing my first online course almost a decade ago, desperately waiting for people to sign up. Back then I had absolutely no experience, access to mentors, or a proven system I could follow. It was frustrating to put in so much work and see little tangible results. However, I knew what I wanted to achieve and I kept going in spite of setbacks. I continued to upgrade my content based on the audience's feedback and I produced additional courses. Fast forward nine months and suddenly everything clicked. The gradual accumulation of my consistent effort in spite of the unknown catapulted my online business to generating revenue of five figures per month.

Now, let's discuss the major benefits *you* will gain as an online course author to make sure you keep that fire alive.

INSTANT GLOBAL IMPACT

Decades ago, if you wanted to become a teacher, you would have to find a job at some type of educational institution. It would require you to follow strict rules and regulations with very limited flexibility. To pursue this path, you would be obligated to obtain a relevant academic title.

Alternatively, you could rent a conference room and organize your own events. But that would require paying a rental fee and funding a successful marketing campaign. All of this would translate to a significant risk of failure and potentially losing your investment.

Moreover, executing your plan successfully wouldn't save you from yet another challenge—constantly trading your time for money. In other words, if you wanted to earn more, you would have had to physically do more. Why? Because without automation, the moment you stop working, you stop earning.

Nowadays, you don't need an academic title. You don't need years of teaching experience or a significant amount of money to invest. More importantly, you are no longer confined to solely reaching people in just your city or state. On the contrary, you have the opportunity to positively impact people across the world all at the same time. Nothing beats the awareness that automation allows your content to help more people around the globe—all on autopilot. When you experience it for the first time, you will see that it's one of the best feelings in the world.

DIGITALLY "CLONE" YOURSELF TO CREATE PASSIVE INCOME

Global impact feels noble, but let's face it—it's not just about that. We all have to find ways to provide for ourselves and our families. Most people trade their time for money. The problem is that you cannot scale your time. Sure, you can continuously increase your fees, but you still have to show up to earn every dollar.

I believe in creating products with potential to generate both impact and recurring revenue. Once you establish your online presence and create smart systems you begin to ride the wave of momentum. For example, thanks to my existing online audience, whenever I want to promote a new, high-quality product, I have immediate, no-cost access to my target viewer.

Your online course allows you to digitally "clone" yourself. It may sound strange, but it really feels as if I have thousands of clones who possess my exact knowledge and experiences, all working for me 24/7. Sometimes when I check my course dashboard after waking up I find that, while I was sleeping, hundreds (sometimes thousands) of people watched my videos. I log into my instructor page and see new reviews, comments, and questions from all corners of the world. And the best part is—all of this happens on autopilot regardless of what I am doing. I know that for you this reality may seem so distant, but I'm the living proof that you can do it too, even if you're starting from zero (like I did).

You may be thinking now: "But, Jimmy, one-to-one coaching can be very fulfilling, and in-person workshops provide immense value." I completely understand. To this day, I do in-person training for companies internationally, including Fortune 500 companies, and occasionally provide personal coaching and consulting. There's no reason you can't continue to embrace those endeavors. However, thanks to the ability to scale your impact through your online courses, you'll be able to do these other endeavors on your terms and with an abundance mindset.

By creating well-performing online products, you'll build a financial foundation that gives you the freedom to choose which clients need 1:1 attention. Finally, you will have the freedom to say "No" to low-priced coaching sessions that keep you scrambling for more work. You'll be able to consult with just the companies and entrepreneurs who value your time and are willing to pay for top service. Creating financial abundance in your life is a game changer.

Building an online empire gives you massive leverage to run your business on *your* terms. You may be shocked when at some point, instead of trying to land new clients, they will be seeking you out.

THE COMMON MISCONCEPTION ABOUT PASSIVE INCOME

Now, I don't mean to be a party pooper, but I need to tell you about a common trap you can fall into. Many people make the erroneous assumption that their first course will do all the work by itself. They simply "dump" it on the web and hope for the best. Some individuals go as far as to repurpose raw webinar recordings without bothering to customize them to fit the online course format. If this approach really worked, everyone would be getting rich. I'm not here to sell you a "get-rich-quick" scam. We all know that attaining any valuable objective requires effort and dedication. Building an online course is no exception.

Generating substantial passive income is an attainable goal, but making it a reality requires a legitimate upfront investment in terms of your time and effort. It's like a merry-go-round. Initially, you pull at it very hard, but once it reaches a certain velocity, it keeps spinning by itself. However, if you don't add little pushes here and there (course updates, audience interaction, creating new programs), it will eventually slow down and at some point lose all the momentum. If you take course creation seriously, build compelling content, and follow my process before, during, and after launch, it will be hard NOT TO succeed to some degree.

Consider that a high-quality course can serve as a driver for you to generate income elsewhere. It's similar to publishing a book. While few writers earn a decent amount of recurring revenue from book sales, many develop a sustainable career by charging consulting and/or speaking fees. The book serves as a tool for them to connect, reach, and inspire clients, but the income can extend far beyond the book sales.

LOCATION INDEPENDENCE

Building a location-independent enterprise can give you the freedom to make a living no matter what unexpected turns life delivers. If you are a coach, consultant, teacher, lawyer, or any other expert, you shouldn't focus solely on trading time for money in a fixed location. Whatever your profession is, imagine having the ability to make a living from the comfort of your home. In reality, you don't even need to be at home. As long as you have your laptop and internet connection, you could be "doing your thing" anywhere on the planet.

As an adventurer, location independence is something I cherish. Over the last ten years I've explored remote locations from the jungles of Colombia to the mountains of Nepal to the surfing beaches of Hawaii. Building an online business has served as the foundation for my globetrotting lifestyle and has led to many exciting opportunities, from running in-company training programs, organizing multi-day adventure masterminds in locations such as the Himalayas, to speaking on international stages. It's incredible to be able to work from anywhere and on my own terms. If that sounds appealing to you, I'm living proof that the possibilities are endless.

TEACHING IS THE BEST FORM OF LEARNING

We don't fully understand something unless we can teach it. In the process of teaching, you will become aware of little gaps in your knowledge that you have to fill in. You will internalize so much more information while designing your content and shooting videos. All of this will positively impact other areas of your life.

- You'll learn how to present your ideas clearly and compellingly.
- Your verbal fluency will skyrocket.
- You'll gain valuable leadership skills that come from actively taking responsibility to educate others.
- You'll rise to the top of your game by getting into and staying in the "arena."

These are personal gains that money can't buy. For example, thanks to my now vast experience in video presenting, I find it easy to speak in front of large audiences—something that used to terrify me. Building courses made me especially proficient in calibrating how long my speeches run. Today, you can give me a topic and a time limit, and I can instantly deliver a presentation from the top of my head. Thanks to the instinct I've cultivated over the years, I can usually finish right on time without even looking at the clock. It's not a talent. It's pure practice. And if you genuinely want it, you will get there too.

LEGACY

I'll never forget when I saw my grandpa Tadeusz lying on the hospital bed. It was hard to admit it, but we all knew the end was coming soon. I was just a teenager and can still vividly remember that scene. I recall the pain of helplessness I felt.

My grandfather was a good man. He was positive and always smiling despite a very challenging life. In his late teens he didn't have the opportunity to chase girls and live the life of a carefree teenager. When the Second World War hit, he had no choice but to join the army. My grandpa spent six years defending his country from the invasion that would end up claiming almost 100 million lives. He even fought in the infamous Monte Cassino battle. Once the war ended, other challenges were awaiting. Due to stress and a poor lifestyle, Tadeusz suffered from a heart attack, then from a stroke that left half of his body paralyzed. As a consequence, he lost the ability to speak clearly. His mental capacity was there, but he wasn't able to fully express himself.

One of the favorite questions of many podcast hosts is: "If you could have dinner with anybody, dead or alive, who would it be?" For me, the answer is obvious—my grandpa. I can't even describe how badly I'd like to have an in-depth conversation with him. I would give a lot to be able to read his book or to see him sharing his ideas, even if it was just a video. Unfortunately, none of that is possible, and my grandpa will always remain somewhat of a mystery to me. Now, you may be wondering: "OK, Jimmy, this is a moving story, but... what does your dead grandpa have to do with course creation?"

Well, as you can see, my grandpa didn't have much choice in life. But you do. Nowadays, it's easier than ever to share your wisdom with the world. Think about it. An average smartphone today has better camera quality than high-budget movie equipment three decades ago. Moreover, with just a few clicks you can get your content out there for the world to see.

Is there a legacy that YOU would like to leave behind when you are gone? What I love about creating courses is that if I die prematurely, my content will keep working 24/7. Think about it, no matter what happens, your kids and future grandkids will be able to get to know you even when you are no longer around. It's a blessing to be aware that your wisdom, experiences, and knowledge will not die with you. Your "digital self" will keep helping others. Moreover, if all goes as planned, your family will keep receiving passive income from the sales of your products. A crazy thought, isn't it? Let it sink in. Even if you die, everything you built will keep providing all types of value. It's a real blessing, and many aspiring content creators never ponder it.

As you can see, building an online course is more than just "banging out a bunch of videos." If you do it right, your course can contribute to your legacy long after you're gone.

BRANDING ON STEROIDS

The way branding works has radically shifted in recent years. Having an online brand is no longer a matter of choice. Whether you want it or not, you already have a personal brand. Let me explain by showing you an example. Imagine that you are attending some type of event. After countless surface interactions, you finally meet several individuals you resonate with. At some point during the conversation, the dots start to connect, and you realize that there could be some potential for collaboration. Suddenly, you hear the announcement that the next speaker is about to begin their keynote. You swiftly exchange business cards and say your goodbyes. Once the event is over, you go back to your hotel room, empty your pockets, and notice several cards that remind you of today's encounters. My question is: What will you do now?

If you are socially savvy, you'll probably spend some time writing short follow-up emails or social media messages. However, you're also very likely to get curious. It's that curiosity that propels most people to Google their new acquaintances.

I know most people don't want to admit it, but they do Google one another. Apart from genuine interest, they want to gauge the status of people they just met, especially in a business context. Are they credible? Are they successful? Do they have testimonials or a large following? Does their brand feel legitimate? These are all valid questions.

If you are considering a new business relationship, it's especially wise to do your due diligence. However, this principle works both ways. People *will* investigate your digital footprint. The billion-dollar question is: What will they see, and how will your online presence make them feel?

ACTION STEP: GOOGLE YOURSELF

I want you to take a short break from reading this book. Go ahead, open the incognito browser on your phone or laptop and Google your name. I want you to look at the results through the eyes of your potential business partners or clients. Ask yourself with full honesty: Is this how I want to be perceived?

You may be satisfied with what you see. If that's the case, ask yourself: "Can I make my online brand even more powerful?" Your first "digital impression" will have an impact on how people perceive you. Therefore, you shouldn't leave it to chance. Why not optimize what people see to increase your probability of winning that client or partnership?

Having a solid video presence online will help you tremendously. Try this thought experiment. Imagine that you searched for someone and stumbled upon a well-presented, high-value video series on YouTube. How would it make you feel? Is it safe to assume that you would think: "Wow, this person must really be an expert in their field. Besides, it takes a lot of courage and discipline to publish a series like this…"

Would you like people to think the same thing when they search your name? What about adding some "steroids" (with no adverse effects) to the impression you make? When you publish a full-blown video course and optimize it well, you can take your online brand to the next level. Imagine what potential clients would think about you when they see all the stats on your course's landing page. For example, how would it make them feel that your two-hour video course has 1,200 students and 47 certified five-star ratings?

Similar to publishing a book, having a high-quality online class delivers tremendous credibility. This in itself is proof that you have the expert knowledge, discipline, and perseverance to make big things happen. After all, you started and completed a process that most people wouldn't feel ready or courageous enough to embark on. This suddenly positions you in the top one percent of experts in your field.

COURSE AS LEVERAGE FOR OTHER ONLINE VENTURES

Your course will become a vital part of your online ecosystem. If you have an existing online presence, publishing a class will only make it stronger. It doesn't matter if you are primarily sharing your content on Instagram, YouTube, blogs, or other platforms. Perhaps you focus on running webinars or Zoom coaching. What matters is that having a course will give you an immense boost of credibility as well as drive traffic to other platforms.

Are you getting exhilarated just by reading this? Good. Let's start turning this excitement into your inner drive, which will keep pushing you forward no matter what. If you already get a lot of value from this book, share your most significant takeaway on LinkedIn or in an Instagram post/story. Make sure to tag @jimmynaraine, as I have a special surprise for those who share the picture of this book.

THINGS TO REMEMBER

- If you only focus on all the work ahead of you, you will likely get overwhelmed. Instead, let your vision fuel you.

- Define a compelling WHY and list all the benefits of building a course.

- Stop trading time for money, and generate a passive income that will allow you to choose only projects and clients you resonate with.

- Your online course will positively impact people on autopilot, transcending geographical barriers while giving you location independence.

- Teaching is the best form of learning.

- Your digital footprint will become your legacy.

- Commit to investing significant time and effort upfront to ensure long-term success and sustainability in your online course business.

- Leverage your online courses as a launchpad for other income opportunities, like consulting or speaking engagements.

- Leave a lasting legacy and benefit future generations by sharing your knowledge and experiences.

CHAPTER 5

TEN HIDDEN WINS FROM AN ONLINE COURSE

We've looked at the "big picture" reasons for building an online course, but there are many "hidden" benefits from having an online course. Here are ten of them.

1) FREE MARKETING

Publishing a high-quality online course is like having an ongoing marketing campaign for your brand that your customers, not you, end up paying for. Once your course is live, it exposes your overall brand to potential clients even while you sleep.

2) ABLE TO PROMOTE A LIVE WORKSHOP OR EVENT

You can design your online course in such a way that it directly (or indirectly) promotes related events. Your course content will serve as a considerable credibility boost when potential attendees search your name on Google. As well, you can promote your event business within your lectures, for instance by sharing relevant case studies from your events or perhaps even directly inviting your students to join you live.

3) CREATE A MASTERMIND GROUP, BOTH OFFLINE OR ONLINE

In 2017, my business partner Alex T. Steffen and I began organizing unforgettable adventures blended with business masterminds in places such as the Himalayas, Canary Islands, Bali, Brazil, and Colombia. Here's the kicker. Having bestselling online courses made it so much easier to attract qualified participants. Instead of constantly stressing about seeking the right people, qualified candidates came to us. Keep this in mind if you want to start running your own mastermind group. Whether it's an online or offline endeavor, becoming a course author will undoubtedly help you advance your plans.

4) DRAMATICALLY INCREASE YOUR FREELANCE FEES

If you are a freelancer, having a well-positioned online course presents you as an industry expert. Increased credibility will help you to land more well-paid gigs. For example, you may be primarily using a freelancing platform such as Upwork. Imagine how valuable it will be to mention your highly-rated course when submitting job proposals. In fact, I encourage you to offer your potential clients free access to your course in order to see if they resonate with your style. First of all, this will make you stand out from your competition right away. Secondly, it shows confidence. And third, due to the reciprocity effect you are more likely to be considered for the job.

5) LAND SPEAKING GIGS

Similarly to being a book author, having a highly-rated course offers you tons of credibility. To get booked on nearly any speaking gig you have to have some form of published video content. Consider that one of the biggest fears of any conference organizer is that speakers they select won't deliver due to stress or poor presentation skills. Having an online video course in your arsenal makes it easier for the organizers to justify choosing you as a speaker. It serves as proof that you can manage your emotions under the pressure of performance. Also, they can get an immediate impression of your presentation style and determine if you are the type of person they are looking for.

6) BUILD CONSULTING AND COACHING SERVICES

For the same reasons I outlined above, it's incredible how much easier it is to land coaching and consulting work after publishing a high-quality online course. In fact, if this is your main priority, you could proactively share your coaching case studies when making video lectures. This offers two benefits. On the one hand, you provide a ton of value. On the other hand, your viewers get a subconscious understanding that perhaps you are the coach they have been searching for.

7) BRING AWARENESS TO A NEW BUSINESS YOU MAY BE LAUNCHING

You can bring awareness to business initiatives by briefly mentioning your new offering at some point in the course (but making sure you don't dilute your content by sounding overly promotional). You can do it indirectly by cleverly "plugging" your new product or service into one of your stories or case studies. This way you educate your audience, giving them something of value while making them aware of your new offering.

8) REINVENT YOURSELF

Starting a career in a new field is daunting. It takes time to learn the ropes and build a name for yourself. A quality online course serves as a springboard to dramatically cut your progress curve and build instant credibility.

9) BUILD A FOUNDATION TO SELL A BOOK

If you are planning to write a book, having an online course can be instrumental to your success. In addition to the credibility and social proof it generates, people who are familiar with your videos are more likely to purchase your book. In fact, you can run a pre-launch book campaign directed at your existing online course audience. This can give you instant traction on book launch day and potentially score excellent early reviews from your core fans. If you bought this book BECAUSE you took one of my courses, you must be smiling now:) (and I'd like to thank you for your continued support).

10) PROMOTE SOMEONE ELSE'S PRODUCT

This is how affiliate marketing works. You promote someone else's product or service and receive a percentage of each sale you generate. For example, lots of content creators in the fitness industry collect affiliate commissions by promoting equipment and health products. It's important to point out that this form of marketing is not allowed on certain platforms and since terms and conditions are never set in stone, make sure you always stay up to date.

ACTION STEP: WHAT'S IN IT FOR YOU?

Now that you have a comprehensive understanding of all the many opportunities you can potentially capitalize on, I invite you to take a piece of paper and start jotting down every single benefit you could possibly derive from your online course. Be as specific as you can. Whether you want to make $9,000 or $190,000 in your first year online, land a specific speaking gig, double your freelancing fees, make your kids proud, impact people in 100+ countries, or prove to yourself that you can... write it all down and don't hold back.

Now is not the time to worry about the "how." We'll cover that later in the book, and I'll provide you with all the tools you need to bring your vision into reality. For now, focus only on your ideal outcome(s). Close your eyes and imagine that you've published your beautiful online course(s). Get in touch with all the positive emotions you would be experiencing. Tune into them right now. Perhaps it's pride, excitement, exhilaration, a feeling of abundance. Maybe it's the realization that you are capable of so much more than you thought.

Write down as many benefits as possible and put that piece of paper in a very visible place, like on your bathroom mirror or a bedroom wall. This will serve as a powerful daily reminder of your "endgame" and will drive you toward your goals, especially when self-doubts start creeping in.

For example, while I was writing the first draft of this book during the Covid lockdown, I could see a whiteboard full of positive affirmations. I placed it directly in front of my desk in order to counter any negative thoughts that might surface from time to time. Some statements on that whiteboard were:

- "My book has helped more than 100,000 people publish their courses."
- "My book helps people to realize that they are good enough."
- "I've received more than 1,000 five-star Amazon reviews from satisfied readers."
- "I'm a best-selling author."
- "Don't judge your writing. Focus on value and keep going."
- "The first draft is meant to suck. Keep going and leave editing for later."

Whenever I had a bad day (and believe me, it happened), I looked up and reminded myself *why* I do what I do. Depending on my mental state, those statements served as a pat on the back or a slap in the face. Either way, they pushed me to keep working on this book until completion. And your WHY can push you to the finish line too.

THINGS TO REMEMBER

- Creating an online course will do wonders for your brand and lead to increased status, more clients, higher fees, and other opportunities.
- Your course can become a marketing machine other people pay for.

- Leverage your course to expand your consulting and coaching services and bolster new business ventures.

- Embrace the power of online courses to reinvent your career, lay the foundation for a bestselling book, and land speaking engagements.

- Jot down ALL potential benefits your online course will give you. Whenever you lack motivation, use this list to rekindle your inner fire.

PART 2

YOUR NICHE & AUDIENCE IDENTIFICATION PHASE

The reticular activating system (also called RAS) is the part of your brain that determines what you focus on. It's a complex network of nerve cells and fibers located in the brainstem. It acts as a gate-keeper for the information that reaches your cerebral cortex (the part of the brain responsible for decision making). Essentially, the RAS helps you pay attention to what should be important to you and filters out the rest. For instance, have you ever been at a mas-sive, overcrowded party, and in spite of very loud music, you man-aged to focus on the conversation you were having with a friend? That's RAS. Or perhaps you got lost in a big crowd as a kid, and in spite of the overall noise, managed to hear your parents calling your name? Thanks again RAS.

How is this relevant to online course creation? Well, we live in a world of constant overstimulation and your potential audience is being bombarded with information 24/7. To be successful in the online space, you need to figure out how to trigger your audience's RAS. In other words, you want your course positioning to be so clear that whenever your target audience sees your course, a light bulb switches on and they have an intense gut reaction of "whatever it is, it was made for me and I need this NOW." I'm sure you've experienced this feeling, the sudden "Eureka!" when you stumble upon something that speaks directly to your soul. Your job is to find an intersection between the audience's needs and your expertise, and create a MUST HAVE product to fill that space.

Deciding what to teach has to be based on more than just a five-second gut decision. You need to figure out not only your subject matter, but also how you will deliver it via a unique angle to a specific audience. In this part of the book, I will help you get clear on your topic within a niche—new or existing— and define the ideal target audience you want to serve. I will share with you the niche and audience identification process I've been refining for a decade. It's comprehensive enough to build a solid foundation and simple enough to prevent you from getting paralyzed.

CHAPTER 6

WHAT TO TEACH IN YOUR FIRST COURSE?

EXPLORING THE POSSIBILITIES

I said it earlier and I'll repeat it here. Being relatable, unique, and enthusiastic are more important than "official" credentials. As long as you have the knowledge, a set of valuable experiences that can help your target audience, and genuine passion for your subject, you can build an impactful course. A lack of genuine enthusiasm will not only hurt your conversion rates, but the customers who do end up purchasing your course will sense your lack of passion. This will certainly lead to refunds and, even worse, negative reviews.

However, even with all the right ingredients in place, deciding what to teach can still be confusing. How do you begin? What's the best way to choose the optimal topic and the specific audience you will serve? Some rare individuals are blessed with complete clarity in this department. However, it's more likely that you find yourself in one of the two following places:

Internal scarcity: You know that you have a calling to share your expertise with the world. However, you also experience a feeling of internal scarcity and have no idea where to begin. Even though you have a deep sense that you have a lot to contribute, you find it incredibly challenging to pinpoint the specifics. You may be fighting an internal battle of feeling like an imposter.

Paradox of choice: You feel trapped in the paradox of choice. There are simply too many things you could share with the world and have absolutely no idea where to begin. You feel overwhelmed by the number of options and tempted to just throw all your knowledge out there in one go.

In the following pages, I will help you gain clarity no matter your primary challenge. I'll share a proven strategy that will serve you well, especially if you experience internal scarcity. Second, we will discuss how to overcome the paradox of choice and make an educated (and clear) decision about your direction. Then we will move on to other important considerations such as niche creation, market research, and last but certainly not least, defining your target audience.

THE "IMPOSSIBILITIES" THAT HAVE ALREADY BECOME YOUR REALITY

If you sometimes feel like you don't have anything to share with the world, I'd like to challenge you. Think about all the things you currently have in your life that once felt impossible. You may have a knee-jerk response along the lines of: "This doesn't apply to me. I've never accomplished anything impossible." However, I want you to think hard. When you analyze your life in a profound and comprehensive manner you will see that you've already turned the impossible into possible.

Perhaps, once upon a time you couldn't speak English, and right now you are reading this book in... English. Maybe your current job/business was just a dream many years ago, and now it's your daily reality. If you currently have a life partner, do you still remember when you got attracted to them for the first time and doubted if you could ever be together? Perhaps there was a specific skill you wanted to develop but learning it seemed insurmountable. Eventually you mastered it and now effortlessly practice it on a daily basis. Have you experienced a major predicament in your life such as trauma, an accident, a death of a loved one, crippling episode or depression, and managed to come out stronger on the other side of it?

I could keep going on, but my point is simple. No matter who you are, you've already turned the impossible into possible in at least one area of your life. Perhaps several. What's more, those experiences fueled you with unique wisdom. It is that wisdom that can positively contribute to other peoples' lives.

YOUR ACTION STEP

Stop here and write down all the "impossibilities" you eventually turned into your reality and all the predicaments you've managed to overcome. If you struggle with internal scarcity, this list will serve as a fertile ground for finding your course subject. It will serve as the living proof that you already have a course, or perhaps, even multiple courses, in you. You just need an extra push to realize that you have what it takes. Always remember that teaching is not about knowing everything. It is about being several steps ahead of your audience and utilizing your unique experience to speed up their progress.

OVERCOME THE PARADOX OF CHOICE

On the flip side, what do you do if there are "too many" things you could teach? How do you get yourself unstuck from overthinking, and commit to a specific path? My answer is simple. Stop treating your first course as a life-or-death matter. It is not. Remember that there is no limit to how many courses you can produce. Rather than allow toxic perfectionism to trap you, realize you need to start somewhere. Commit to one, specific topic. You can publish more courses later, but after completing one at least you will have some real-life experience under your belt.

Also, unless you already have an existing audience, assume that one course will not be enough. I'm pointing this out since I often meet dreamers who have the notion that just one product will make them rich. Of course, this does happen from time to time and I would love for it to happen to you. Still, many uber-successful course authors already have a solid foundation in place before launching their course. Some have a pre-existing email list, a large following on social media, or joint ventures with influential people. Others are backed with a substantial advertising budget combined with marketing expertise. If you don't have any of those assets, don't worry. You'll just need to use some sweat equity to make up that gap. I'm not saying that you will *not* make a lot of money with one course. You may, and I sincerely hope you do. What I'm saying is that blindly relying on one egg in one basket would be foolish.

I encourage you to take a more holistic approach. Why limit yourself by the idea (and the immense pressure that comes with it) of producing one "perfect" course, if there is no limit to how many courses you can publish? Understanding this will help you to overcome your paradox of choice and make a move.

I started my journey by building a course on Udemy called *Double Your Confidence and Self-Esteem.* When I made my first dollar online it radically shifted my mindset. I went from "I think this is possible" to "I KNOW FOR A FACT that this is possible." And I didn't stop there. I kept building content and listening to the needs of my audience. In the span of my first year online I created six video courses, and that start has been the foundation for my success. You see, course creation is a long game. You have to provide value continually to your audience. That's how you stand out from competitors.

This is good news for those who struggle to choose a topic for their first course. Once you realize that you can (and should) publish multiple courses, you no longer feel the pressure of making the perfect decision on the front end. You're free to just go after one idea at a time.

ARE YOU A SARDINE OR A SHARK?

There is an old saying you may have heard: "Riches are in the niches." This is especially true in today's hectic, overstimulated world. One of the biggest mistakes new course creators make is trying to package everything they know into one course and sell it to the mainstream, rather than concentrating on generating excellent results for a well-defined, niche audience. Avoid the (completely natural) temptation to "unload" everything you want to teach into one course. More doesn't mean better. When people buy courses, they crave practical solutions to specific problems, not huge quantities of generalized information.

If you were in danger of losing your eyesight, would you rather consult with a general practitioner or an experienced eye specialist? The answer is obvious. All of us have more trust in niche experts. When I talk about this concept, people often retort: "I have so much knowledge I want to share... I can't just stick to one niche."

Even if you have limitless information to share, it's important to take things one course at a time. When in doubt, analyze your content ideas in the context of your target customer and your course objectives (I will take you through my full process in Part 3). If the content is not applicable, keep it for a future course. "Kill your darlings" is common advice from experienced book authors. What it means is that you need to cut your content ruthlessly whenever something is not relevant. This applies to course creation as well.

While there is a time and place for creating courses on broad topics, it's not the best option if you are just starting out. Unless you are fully committed to building a premium masterclass for a well-established following, it's wiser to become a shark in a smaller niche versus a tiny sardine trying to survive in a vast ocean. Aim to stand out from your competition by focusing on a very specific angle that you resonate with. Let's look at some examples.

Maybe you always felt incapable of learning technology but eventually taught yourself how to create websites. If this is your experience, instead of building a ten-hour-long, complicated web design course targeting everyone, you could focus on primarily teaching those who are not tech-savvy. In this case, you could create a three-hour class showcasing only the fundamentals, using simple language, and always keeping in mind that your target customer doesn't feel comfortable with technology. The potential course title could be: "Web Design for the Technologically Challenged," or "Ten Steps to Build a Website Without Breaking a Sweat."

If you are a yoga teacher who previously worked for an investment bank, you could capitalize on that experience. After all, you still vividly remember how hectic the life of a banker is. Instead of building another long and generic yoga course that could get easily lost on the web, you could focus on a niche yoga course for ultra-busy professionals. For example: *"Seven-Minute Yoga for Busy CEOs"* or something more funky such as *"Say Bye to Stress and Hi to Zen with Seven-Minute Yoga."*

We could come up with other examples all night long, but I'm sure you see my point. Never look at your topic choice through a black or white lens. There are many different shades (certainly more than 50) you can focus on.

In the next chapter we'll discuss another critical ingredient that most people rarely consider: defining your **ideal target customer**.

THINGS TO REMEMBER

- Overcome internal scarcity by recognizing all your past achievements. You have already turned "impossibilities" into reality.

- Overcome the paradox of choice by constantly reminding yourself that your first course isn't a make-or-break decision.

- Don't fall for the "one perfect course" trap. Acknowledge that there's no limit to the number of courses you can create, and focus on providing continuous value to your audience.

- Choose a well-defined niche and stand out as a shark rather than settling for being a sardine.

- Capitalize on your unique background and experiences to offer specific solutions for targeted audiences.

- Rigorously cut out irrelevant content and focus on practical, step-by-step solutions, concentrating on the needs of your ideal target customer.

CHAPTER 7

DEFINE YOUR IDEAL AUDIENCE

WHO IS YOUR IDEAL CUSTOMER?

We've already established that going broad rarely works. One key to becoming a shark in a small pond is defining your **target audience**. This is a fundamental step in any business, yet most course authors either disregard it or they make the mistake of trying to build content for everyone, convinced that this increases the probability of getting more enrollments. The opposite is usually the case. People want to feel like you are speaking directly to them.

Let's examine the concept of a **customer avatar**. I'd describe a customer avatar as the representation of your ideal future customer based on their attitudes, values, beliefs, desires, fears, and more. You use this fleshed-out avatar to identify your target customer's pain points, characteristics, circumstances, and even the language they use. Once you do this you will find it easier to calibrate your message directly to that predefined customer.

For example, I've been very clear from the beginning that I wrote this book specifically for subject experts who have been dabbling in the idea of producing an online course, but who have been held back by fear, perceived complexity, and/or confusion. Does this mean that other customer groups won't benefit from this guide? Not at all. **Course Creation Simplified** can provide immense value to people from various walks of life, even if they are not in my target audience. A company executive may want to understand content strategy, a journalist may be looking for ways to improve his brand, or a college student may want to overcome the fear of putting herself out there. This book goes beyond a stiff, hands-on course creation guide. Focusing on a specific customer avatar enabled me to sharpen my content and delivery with my target reader always in mind. You can even give your avatar a name. In fact, the more vivid and specific you make your avatar, the more it will help you in calibrating your content.

I recommend that you take this even one step further. I'm sure there's a person or even multiple people in your life who are a perfect representation of your target audience. When you plan, design, and film your course, imagine that you are speaking directly to them. You may prefer to imagine just one person. Or, if it's difficult to identify that one real-life individual who you know who possesses all the characteristics of your customer avatar, it may be easier to think of a mash-up of two or three people you want to help.

While writing this book I envisioned several close friends who have the characteristics of my customer avatar. They're all amazing experts with great gifts to share. Sadly, they also lack confidence and clarity, which in turn has triggered procrastination. I frequently reminded myself that I was writing this book for them.

Whenever I felt stuck, not sure how to address a certain topic, I imagined these friends sitting across from me and asking me for help. This alleviated the pressure (because I know I'm ultimately serving them), but it also helped me remove unnecessary fluff from my writing (because I know they won't stand for any BS). When you focus on creating value for a specific person it allows you to strip down your content to what truly matters.

When Tim Ferriss was working on his first book he imagined typing emails to his friends who were 25 to 40 years old, tech-savvy, San Francisco-based males. For 15 years now his book, *The 4-Hour Workweek*, has helped millions of people from various backgrounds. However, starting his work with a specific niche in mind was key for him to deliver a useful solution to the people whose pain points he was most familiar with. When you focus on one niche and customer avatar, you will create an interesting phenomenon. When someone from your target audience discovers your course, they will have a distinct feeling that you made the course specifically for them. They may even think: "Wow, it seems like [your name here] really understands my current situation. It's incredible. They speak my language!" It will also make them more likely to leave an excellent review and tell their friends to buy your product. Eventually, you may reach a tipping point where an increasing number of individuals who extend beyond your target "customer avatar" start signing up.

I always make it very clear in my promotional materials who my courses are made for. This way, any time an ideal customer stumbles upon my landing page, they can't help but think: "Wow, it looks like this guy made videos exactly for a person like me." This strategy has increased my conversion rates and overall rating, since customers know what to expect right from the start and receive exactly what they need. Just like with Tim Ferriss's book, many of my courses have reached the tipping point, and now, thanks to social proof, people from various walks of life (often very different from my initial customer avatar), sign up.

For example, I have two public speaking courses, each designed for a different audience. One of them is shorter and primarily designed for busy professionals who want to focus on overcoming in the shortest time possible their fear of public speaking. From the very beginning, I make clear that the course isn't about more technical aspects of presenting, such as designing the speech flow or creating slides. The message is simple: if your number one goal is overcoming stage fright and you have little time, take this course. My second, much longer (more than 12 hours) course is designed to be the complete public speaking blueprint for those who are willing and able to dive deep and invest a significant amount of time. In that course my videos are about gaining confidence on stage, creating compelling content, cultivating smooth delivery, inspiring team members and more. Even though the second course offers significantly more content, it doesn't mean that it's inherently better, as different audiences resonate with different formats.

YOUR ACTION STEPS

Before you read further, complete these steps.

Step 1: Define all the characteristics of your target audience, addressing the following questions:

- What are the pain points of my avatar? What are they "struggling" with?
- What is their biggest stumbling block?
- What is missing in the existing courses that seek to address those challenges?
- Why do they care about finding a solution?

- What is one thing that needs to happen for them to feel like they succeeded?
- What are their deepest dreams and desires?
- What examples can they resonate with?
- What are the possible objections they may have?
- What is it about me that they will resonate with?

Step 2: Create a vivid and specific customer avatar. Feel free to give that avatar a name, or even choose people you know who are an accurate representation of your ideal customer. It's really worth investing some quality time to go through this exercise. Surprisingly, even though getting crystal clear on who you want to serve is the foundation of any business success, many people never take that step. When you are in the process of creating your course, always keep your avatar(s) in mind in order to better calibrate your approach.

# # #

TAP INTO THE SOURCE

If you've set your mind on becoming truly successful in the online course space, I encourage you to take one more (often uncomfortable) step. What I'm about to propose is something that less than 1% of aspiring creators will ever attempt, but it's a simple way to get an edge. It's this: Actually *talk* to your target audience to get a deeper understanding of what makes them tick. This is the best way to test your assumptions and further calibrate your content and delivery. When you want to learn about your audience, the best teacher is... your audience.

How do you find your ideal audience? First, the chances are that you already have people in your life who are an accurate representation of your avatar. Second, ask yourself, "Where does my audience like to hang out?" and then join those circles, whether it's an in-person gathering or an online group. Offer those individuals value with no strings attached. Figure out exactly what they struggle with and how you can support them. Make sure to take plenty of notes along the way, paying attention to key phrases you keep hearing. The reason is that by talking to your avatars you will not only get a deeper understanding of their challenges, but you'll also discover how to "speak their language." Tapping into their internal dialog will make creating your curriculum, and especially your sales copy, much easier.

Let's consider an example. If your customer avatar is a female entrepreneur who wants to become a more powerful negotiator, you may hear them repeat certain phrases. For instance: "I sometimes feel like an imposter," or "Those self-proclaimed alpha guys often speak over me and I don't know how to handle it," or "I need to be more assertive, but I'm too nice," or "I'm tired of feeling like a pushover." You could then use those hot phrases when creating your promotional material to trigger an emotional response. In this example, you could start your trailer (I will teach you all about trailers later) video with the following:

> "Are you a female entrepreneur sick and tired of letting others push you around during negotiation? Do people sometimes take advantage of you simply because you are too nice? Do you find it difficult to be assertive when negotiating with overbearing, self-proclaimed 'Alpha males'? Perhaps you sometimes feel like an imposter? The good news is that all of those challenges can be solved."

By tapping into the internal dialog of your customer avatar you make their RAS pay immediate attention. You trigger the feeling of: "This sounds just like me. It's like this person is reading my mind. I need to look into this course ASAP!"

Please remember that this strategy is about more than just calibrating your promotional material for more sales. First and foremost, it is about deepening your understanding of your audience so you are more equipped to solve their biggest challenges.

THINGS TO REMEMBER

- People want to feel that you speak directly to them rather than AT them.

- Define your target audience by creating a detailed customer avatar distinguishing their specific characteristics, desires, and pain points.

- Focusing on creating value for a specific person allows you to strip down your content to what truly matters.

- In your promotional materials, explain clearly who your course serves to ensure you attract the correct audience. Otherwise, you risk getting negative ratings and refunds from those who feel tricked into investing in something they weren't looking for.

- Talk to your potential customers to learn how to calibrate your content and delivery using the language they resonate with.

- When creating promotional materials, use key phrases from conversations with your avatar to trigger an emotional response.

CHAPTER 8

DON'T ASSUME.
TEST AND OPTIMIZE.

At this point you've decided on the topic you want to pursue, and you've identified your target audience. However, before you start designing your course, you must analyze the current market. The tools built into the contemporary online space enable you to test virtually any idea, any time, and on any (or no) budget. Instead of blithely assuming that there is a demand for the specific course you plan to teach, first analyze the market, test your idea, and then optimize your course based on your findings. While approaching a decision about a specific angle you will tackle, make sure there is a corresponding need in today's market and that people are willing to pay for your solution to their problems. You shouldn't rely just on your gut feeling. Instead, utilize online tools to gauge which topics are in demand and how your competition meets those needs.

Whether you are planning to publish your course on Udemy or not, I recommend playing around with their native tool called **Marketplace Insights.** Housed directly on Udemy's site, this tool will show you which topics are most successful and how much money top courses in your category earn. Please bear in mind that the estimated revenue doesn't include the income from the Udemy for Business collection, which is a corporate subscription model that can be very lucrative (more about it in part 5). You'll also be able to identify top instructors in various categories, which will enable you to study your competition very carefully.

Accessing this tool is very simple and using it is straightforward:

1. Create a free instructor account on Udemy.

2. Go to your **dashboard** and click on **Tools,** then **Marketplace Insights**.

Remember, you can always refer to my resources page for updated links, checklists, and other resources: **www.jimmynaraine. com/coursecreationresources**

COMPETITOR ANALYSIS

When you explore Marketplace Insights, I strongly encourage you to take the time to determine what makes certain courses successful and also identify their weaknesses. Pick several high-performing courses and analyze their landing pages, curriculum, and promotional videos. Figure out what is working well, but also ask yourself: "Is there room for improvement? How can I provide more value than my competition?"

One great strategy is to read your competition's customer ratings and look for patterns. This direct feedback from customers will give you a better understanding of what people find lacking in existing course content. I encourage you to collate the most common feedback into a spreadsheet for enhanced clarity. You can then figure out how to fill those missing pieces in your course(s). For instance, if many students complain that your competition doesn't provide any supplementary written material, it may be an indication you should create PDF summaries in your course to address that unfulfilled need.

Naturally, you may go all in and enroll in some of the top-performing courses in your niche to conduct an in-depth analysis. This strategy can be eye-opening, but sadly, it can also serve as a procrastination mechanism. In other words, you may spend weeks or months analyzing other peoples' content to secretly justify not pulling the trigger on your course.

TEST YOUR CONTENT EARLY

Once you've got a solid understanding of the existing course market, including your competition's strengths and weaknesses, I recommend testing your ideas. One easy way to do this is to create a series of social media posts on topics you are considering. You can shoot a short video series with your selected tips to see how they perform. You can see how real people respond to your content.

For instance, this is precisely what my friend Jason Goldberg did to test various content ideas for his upcoming online course. Jason is a bestselling author, an accomplished stage host, and a former rapper (who once opened for the Wutang Clan!), and he has been running his successful coaching practice for years. With his resume, it would've been easy to fall into the ego trap and assume that he understood his audience completely. However, he religiously tested his assumptions instead of blindly believing them. To do it, Jason scheduled a series of LIVE Q&A videos tackling various subjects. To his surprise, some topics that received the most significant engagement were initially very low on his priority list, and vice versa. This is a valuable lesson for all of us. If you genuinely want to know what makes your audience tick and what they crave, take the time to talk to them and test various ideas.

THE FLIPSIDE OF TESTING

Proper testing can save you a ton of time in the long run, as it will help you to choose the right niche. However, the potential danger is that you may treat it as a procrastination tool and end up squandering all your time on social media. For this reason, unless you're committed to building an extensive masterclass, I recommend giving yourself no more than 2 weeks to test your idea.

MY OPTIMAL FORMULA FOR TESTING

Instead of falling victim to one of two extremes (publishing without testing or triggering procrastination by testing too much), there is a better way. Namely, once you analyze your competition, talk to your customer avatar, and perform the first set of tests on social media. Then go ahead, and finalize your tests by publishing... an actual course. However, I am not referring to creating a comprehensive masterclass. Instead, I like to build 40 to 60-minute concise yet powerful online courses to gauge my audience's reaction. The strategy is to keep my eyes and ears open to early feedback and improve my programs based on it. Thanks to this approach, I am, in a way, co-creating my course content with my audience.

Also, instead of putting all my chips on one digital product, this approach allows me to test multiple course ideas and angles quickly. According to the 80/20 principle, most results come from a minority of inputs. Essentially, very few things really matter, and my job here is to identify which courses have the most potential.

When I identify one of those winning "horses," I invest a lot of extra time and effort into adding new material.

For instance, several years ago, I published a course called: 40-min Confidence Guide, and it was precisely that - merely 40 minutes of video lectures about confidence. However, I kept adding more content since the early feedback was promising. As traffic to my landing page and conversion rates increased, I added even more content. In 2023, the course that was initially 40 minutes long has over 5 hours of content, and to this day is my top-seller. However, to find one massive winner, you sometimes need to test various ideas being comfortable with the fact that statistically, some of them will fail.

Now that you know your topic angle, the target audience, and have a solid foundation in place, let's start building your course. In Part 3 we will discuss how to structure your course and design content so people find it irresistible.

THINGS TO REMEMBER

- Perform competitor analysis by examining successful courses, identifying strengths and weaknesses, and using customer ratings to uncover areas for improvement.

- Test your content ideas early by creating social media posts, short video series, or live Q&A sessions to gauge audience interest and engagement. Adapt your course material accordingly.

- Set a maximum two-week testing window to avoid procrastination and maintain a balance between gathering insights and moving forward with your course.

- Develop concise, 40-60 minute courses to test the audience's reaction. Identify the most promising courses based on early feedback, then refine and expand the material.

- Apply the 80/20 principle to identify courses with the most potential and invest additional time and effort into improving them.

- Accept that some course ideas will fail and focus on refining successful ones to maximize impact.Analyze the online course market using tools like Udemy's Marketplace Insights to identify in-demand topics.

PART 3

BLUEPRINT FOR CREATING WORLD-CLASS CONTENT

The Inner Dialog of an Aspiring Course Author:

I've just watched one hour of inspirational videos and I feel fired up. I can't wait to get started on building my course. It's going to be epic. All right, I will watch just one more video and then get started.

(One hour later)

Okay, I better get off YouTube and finally do something before my energy goes away. Okay, screw it. I'm ready. What should I begin with, though? Aaaah, I know, I'm going to brainstorm the content.

(20 minutes later).

I have so many ideas, how on earth do I put them together? <Deep sigh> Okay, okay, I'm overthinking. I'll just focus on the first video for now.

(45 minutes later)

The notes I've just made seem decent, but I'm not sure if they relate to the course's premise. Actually, what is my premise? <long blank stare> I'm not entirely sure. It's so complicated. What if I'm wasting my time?

(25 minutes later)

Ohhh I'm stuck. My mind feels cloudy. Maybe it's the caffeine crash. Yeah, that must be it. Damn. I won't be able to work on this today. All this time and energy for nothing, like a loser. Hmmm... I know, I'm going to at least make an Instagram post. It's good for the business, and it's simple.

# # #

Does this sound familiar? Well, it does to me! I was a victim of this negative loop many times. The biggest danger of falling into this unproductive pattern is not merely the time you end up wasting. After all, each one of us sometimes experiences the heaviness of bad days. The biggest issue is that situations like this reinforce your limiting belief that course creation is too complicated AND that you are not good enough.

Benjamin Franklin was right when he said that "failing to plan is planning to fail." If you don't have a solid plan of action, a blueprint, you are making it very difficult for yourself to succeed. Instead of focusing your creative energy on clean and well-targeted execution, you end up wasting a lot of mental resources on worrying, getting stuck, and trying to get unstuck. Your lack of a clear strategy increases perceived complexity, which in turn triggers pro-crastination.

How do most content creators react when procrastination shows its ugly face? Well, many times it's by producing small pieces of content here and there, whether it's social media articles, Instagram photos, or short video stories. All of those actions make them feel like they are doing something important. However, it's really wasted time. They stay busy winning tiny battles without ever going to war. Instead of working on publishing a high-quality online course, they dabble in distractions. In case you're wondering, I've been there too.

Here's a question that puts things in perspective: Would you embark on a long solo adventure in the Himalayas without a solid game plan? I love trekking in Nepal and assure you that hitting the trails without a plan could easily cost you your life. You may be thinking, hey, building a course is far from a life-or-death situation. I could argue it's similar—are you truly living if you keep your un-realized dreams bottled up inside you? Creating your first course is not merely about dropping a bunch of content online. It's about climbing your personal Everest.

In this part of the book, I will show you exactly how to design a captivating course, from A to Z. You are about to discover the proven process I've been refining for almost a decade as I created 40 courses for half a million people.

Now that you've chosen your topic and clarified what specific audience you will serve, we can progress to designing your course. You will learn how to structure your course in a smart way to max-imize conversions and deliver value to your customers. We will also delve deep into the process of creating all the building blocks of your course. We will then examine the vital ingredients that make content captivating and transformative. The more effort you put into this phase of your online course creation adventure, the easier it will be for you to shoot the actual videos. So fasten your seatbelt and let the ride begin.

CHAPTER 9

FUNDAMENTALS OF YOUR COURSE LANDING PAGE

Let's begin by talking about what your landing page actually is and how it should be structured. The **landing page** is a destination webpage where your online course is hosted. It provides all the information that potential users need to know about your course, including the promotional material to entice them to enroll. The quality of your landing page will determine people's first impression, hence it is essential to make it as compelling as possible. For instance, here are examples of my Udemy landing pages: **https://www.udemy.com/user/jimmynaraine/**

If you've ever purchased an online course, a book, or an audio program, you did it via a landing page. For instance, it's likely that you bought this very book from my Amazon destination page. When you build your online course, you need to put a lot of thought into creating a compelling landing page. The equation is simple: The better the landing page, the higher the probability that people will purchase your product.

The vital ingredients of any course landing page include:

- Captivating title and subtitle.
- Promotional video (also called a trailer).
- Course objectives.
- Description.
- Curriculum.
- Call to action (CTA) to get them to click on the "buy" button.
- Money-back guarantee (optional).
- Your bio.
- Customer reviews.

While the structure may differ based on various factors, this is how I design all my landing pages. Also, it's something that **Udemy. com** recommends based on their experience of working with tens of thousands of instructors and 56 million students.

I will break down some of the above elements later in this part. Also, to further simplify the process, I created a bonus video for you where I walk you through a landing page set up, explaining why various pieces are essential and how they work together. You can find the tutorial on my resources page: **www.jimmynaraine. com/onlinecourseresources**

Having said that, the best way to get a real feeling for what a landing page is all about is to set up a free instructor account on one of the online course platforms (I'll break them down in Part 5). Whether you plan to publish on Udemy.com or not, I feel like they have the easiest course dashboard to navigate and create a mock course. You can create a draft landing page in literally just a few clicks and then preview how it will appear to your potential customers.

THINGS TO REMEMBER

- A landing page is your online course's destination web-page providing all necessary information and promotional material to entice users to enroll.

- Essential elements of a course landing page include a captivating title and subtitle, promotional video, course objectives, description, curriculum, call to action, money-back guarantee (optional), your bio, and customer reviews.

- Please set up a free instructor account on an online course platform (e.g., Udemy) to create and preview a draft landing page and familiarize yourself with its structure and features.

CHAPTER 10

YOUR ONLINE COURSE STRUCTURE

It's important to know what it takes to create an effective, well-designed landing page, but the work doesn't stop there. You then need to carefully structure your course and outline the content. Let's walk through the process together, step-by-step, starting with an overview of the essential building blocks of your online course:

1. Course introduction video.

2. Multiple content videos divided into sections.

3. Separate introduction to each section.

4. Conclusion video.

5. Promotional video (trailer).

6. Bonus lectures.

Some authors (including myself) also add supplementary material. That's not a must, but I highly recommend it. Those additional resources may include quizzes, PDF summaries, printouts, Excel sheets, coding exercises, assignments, infographics, interactive activities, templates, audio files, and more. There is no right or wrong material to include, and what you decide to include depends on your subject matter, style, and what your audience resonates with.

Now, let's break down each element of the course structure and look at how to make it captivating and value-driven.

COURSE INTRODUCTION VIDEO

The **introduction video** is a vital element of any decent course, but many creators forget about this step. Sure, the world won't end if you dive into the core content without introducing yourself and your course first. However, your viewers will be left wondering who you are, the best practices for taking your course, how to get more bang for their buck, etc. They'll feel as if they're embarking on a journey without first looking at the map.

I like to start my introduction videos by expressing my appreciation for their decision to enroll. I greet everyone in an upbeat manner, say a few relevant things about myself, share some tips for making the most of the course, and explain exactly what they are about to learn. The easiest way to plan the introduction video is to imagine that you are about to teach a live class. Jot down all the things students need to know before getting started, and base your introduction video on those points. Here are some ingredients you can use:

- Warm welcome.
- Short introduction of who you are and why you teach.
- Best practices for making the most of the course.

- Course objectives.

- Invitation to introduce themselves (or other call to action to boost engagement).

- Encourage them to ask questions whenever they are in doubt.

You can also make a separate video in which you share your full story. The reason you should consider this is because many people are curious about their instructor. This may apply more with some topics than with others. For instance, if you are teaching something that you used to struggle with yourself, such as overcoming social anxiety or moving from employment to entrepreneurship, it makes sense to share your personal story of overcoming that challenge. On the other hand, if you're teaching a technical skill like how to create powerful Excel spreadsheets, this type of personal video may not be necessary. Ultimately, it's your call.

I recommend that if you decide to make a separate video introducing yourself, let people know it's optional. In fact, I like to add the word "optional" in the video title. I do this because I'm aware that some students won't care about my story, and they'd rather get to the core of the course right away. I want to make sure that they don't feel like they are missing out by not watching the video.

MULTIPLE CONTENT PIECES DIVIDED INTO SECTIONS

While trailers and introduction videos are important, the content videos make up the core of any course. Later in this book, I'll show you how to come up with the curriculum and content for your videos. For now, let's discuss how to structure your videos within a course.

Some of the most common questions people ask me are:

- Should I make several long videos or many shorter ones?
- Should I divide them into sections and, if so, how so?

Even though every situation is different, there are some essential rules you should consider when building your course. Based on my experience, the ideal video length is between 3 and 9 minutes. In less than 3 minutes, it's hard to convey enough value, and after 9 minutes your videos can quickly get overwhelming. Of course, there are exceptions, but if in doubt, stick to the above standards. You should also divide videos into separate course sections that act as different **idea clusters**. This way you make your content more digestible, essentially creating a clear roadmap for your students. We will discuss clusters in more detail when we go through the full step-by-step process later in this part of the book.

"Why not just post several longer videos?" you may ask.

Well, there are several reasons. First, as I already mentioned, longer videos can feel burdensome. Second, the perceived value of your course decreases when you have just a few videos even if they are lengthy. Imagine that you, as a customer, are trying to decide between two similar products. Everything, from the course topic to ratings and even the presenters' charisma are nearly the same. The only difference is the number of videos in the course.

1. The first course has six videos, 20 minutes each.
2. The second course has 20 videos, six minutes each.

What is your perception of value?

Remember, that like most of your potential customers, you're in a hurry and don't want to take too much time to make a decision. Even though the total amount of content is the same (6x20 minutes versus 20x6 minutes), the perception about value can be dramatically different. Your busy brain sees 6 videos versus 20 videos and automatically assigns more perceived value to the course with more content pieces. It may have nothing to do with reality, but that doesn't matter. In the world of marketing, perception presents a new reality. A greater number of videos also suggests that the author put a lot of effort into curriculum design. Instead of "dumping" several long videos on you, they took time to break things down into digestible pieces.

Put yourself in the shoes of your customer. When you see a 20-minute video ahead of you, it's easy to rationalize that you don't have enough time to watch the entire lecture. You are likely to think: "Well, I want to watch it, but I'll do it later." On the other hand, even busy people can justify watching a six-minute lecture. The amazing thing is that watching one single, short lecture will, in most cases, turn into another one, and another one, and then another one. Naturally, this will only happen if your lectures are extremely valuable and this is why, in two chapters from now, we will discuss the necessary ingredients of creating compelling content.

Moreover, one of your goals as a content creator is to maximize the **engagement rate** in your course. This means that you want as many people as possible to watch your content from beginning to end. First, this will increase your impact. Second, those students will be more likely to post excellent reviews, buy more courses, and recommend your work to others. And third, if you use a marketplace platform such as Udemy, a high retention rate will positively impact the algorithm and show your course(s) to more potential buyers.

SEPARATE INTRODUCTION TO EACH SECTION

Creating a separate introduction for each section isn't crucial, but it certainly will be appreciated by your audience. In these intros you can congratulate your viewers for completing the previous sections. Then, you can tell them exactly what they are about to learn next. The purpose of such a video is to make people feel comfortable with their learning path while maintaining high morale and excitement.

If you're teaching a technical topic and rely on screencasts (also called screenshares), section introduction videos are your chance to deepen the connection with your students through a "talking head" video. I realize that showing your face may feel very uncomfortable if you normally don't speak in front of the camera, but it's really worth it. In fact, if this is something that you struggle with, don't worry. In the next part of this book, I will share my powerful strategies to become a more confident presenter. What's more, on my resources page, you can find free bonus videos I made for you about confident presenting: **www.jimmynaraine.com/course creationresource**

CONCLUSION VIDEO

Don't neglect this vital element. Put yourself in the shoes of your customers. They've just completed your entire class, something that most people don't have the patience for. It clearly means that they've become the core "fans" of your content. Now you need to show some appreciation for those people because they form your inner circle. Make a video in which you thank them for their time and their trust in your content. Finish with a positive note, perhaps by sharing an inspiring story.

Your conclusion also serves as an excellent opportunity for you to give them some type of call to action, whether it's asking for a formal review, checking out your other courses, or signing up for your newsletter. *Now is the time to ask.* Everyone likes the feeling they get when they complete something, so the chances are your students will be more likely to act upon your CTA right away.

Speaking of CTAs, if you already feel like you've got a lot of value from this book, I'd appreciate your Amazon review tremendously:) It takes only 60 seconds and will help aspiring course creators discover this book so they, too, can find the courage to share their knowledge with the world. Thank you.

PROMOTIONAL VIDEO (TRAILER)

A high-quality course trailer is vital; it's one of the most powerful factors that will determine your conversion rates. This is why I'm devoting a full chapter to teach you exactly how to create a promotional video that will captivate your prospects and make your course look irresistible.

BONUS

Everyone likes free extras. Giving away bonuses works magic and often serves as a deciding factor when customers choose between two competing products. After all, we love to feel like we scored the best deal. As a course creator, you can use this psychology to increase the perception of your course's value. Instead of publishing only your core curriculum, you can create several bonus lectures that complement your core offering. Make it clear that you are including these lectures as a free bonus to further enhance the value of your online course. I encourage you to give away some bonuses during your launch and then add new ones over time. You may be saying to yourself: "All of this sounds like a lot of work, Jimmy." Well, the good news is that if you carefully plan your content strategy you can pre-create all of your future bonuses in one batch before your launch and then release them over time. More about this later.

THINGS TO REMEMBER

- Essential online course videos are introduction, core lectures, section intros, conclusion, trailer, and bonus lectures.

- Enhance learning with supplementary materials like quizzes, PDF summaries, printouts, and interactive activities.

- The optimal content video length is 3-9 minutes.

- Divide lectures into digestible sections (idea clusters).

- Include section intros to build excitement and give people clarity as to what they will learn.

- Craft a conclusion video to express appreciation, inspire, and offer calls to action.

- Create a captivating trailer and offer bonus lectures to improve conversion rates and increase perceived value.

CHAPTER 11

YOUR PROMOTIONAL VIDEO (TRAILER)

The purpose of a **promo video** (AKA a trailer) is to grab the attention of your ideal customer and show them all the reasons why they need to enroll in your course. Your **trailer** is often the first time your potential customer will see and hear you. This first digital impression is make or break. At the same time, here's an important consideration. We live in a hectic world and we're all constantly bombarded with stimuli. As much as we like to believe that potential buyers will carefully analyze our offer, very few people watch course trailers to the very end. It's often enough for them to see the first minute to determine if they even want to entertain the idea of investing in your course.

Typically what happens is that your trailer "sells" other elements on your landing page. For example, nobody wants to spend their valuable time reading detailed reviews or going through your curriculum unless their buying "temperature" is already high. That's why a captivating trailer is key. It transforms casual browsers into warm prospects. Here are the essential elements of a high-quality trailer:

1. Hook point.
2. Credibility mixed with vulnerability.
3. Clear and compelling benefits for the viewer.
4. Call to action (CTA).
5. Money-back guarantee.

I highly encourage you to go online, find promotional videos that appeal to you, and break them down. You may even want to transcribe the ones that hooked you the most. This process will teach you a lot about what works and what doesn't. I always repeat: There's no point in reinventing the wheel if you can learn from those who have already made things happen. Having said that, don't be afraid to experiment. If you have an idea that you really believe can work, give it a shot and test it out.

THE FIRST ELEMENT: HOOK POINT

In a trailer you need to grab a viewer's attention from the very beginning. People have a very short attention span. If you don't trigger any emotion during the first ten seconds, they will move on to other options.

Many course instructors make the mistake of starting their trailers with a long logo animation or some sort of musical introduction that doesn't provide any value for the viewer. They are shooting themselves in the foot, losing potential customers. When I point out this mistake, the typical justification is that they need to do a long intro as part of their branding. Nobody cares about you or your branding unless you can do something for them. You could have a fantastic logo animation, but what's the point if nobody enrolls in your course? Don't get me wrong. There is a time and place for branding, but not in the first 30 seconds of your trailer. The first part of your promotional video is meant to stand out and capture attention by making your students FEEL something.

It's always a good idea to start your video by triggering emotions in your viewer. Spend some time emphatically talking about the pain and challenges they are experiencing. Make it as vivid and charismatic as possible. Then, show them that you are the one who can help them to alleviate that pain. If you do this effectively you will have their full attention. You'll also make them want to watch the rest of the trailer and read through your entire landing page. All of this increases the probability that they will give your course a shot.

THE SECOND ELEMENT: CREDIBILITY AND VULNERABILITY

Your promo video needs to make it clear why you are qualified to teach your topic. As we discussed previously, that doesn't mean that you need to be the best in the world or have multiple formal qualifications. It just means that the potential buyer needs to know that he or she can trust your content. I'm aware that it may feel a little bit uncomfortable to talk about your accomplishments. However, it's necessary in the context of your chosen topic. If you do this with authenticity nobody will think you are showing off. After all, people want to know why you are qualified to teach them. Put yourself in the shoes of your potential customer. Then, ask yourself: "What gives me the most credibility?" Then go ahead and tell the viewer.

I genuinely believe in the combination of credibility and vulnerability. **Vulnerability** is your willingness to step into the uncomfortable by sharing things that are not easy to admit. It's about authentically embracing your human side. Remember when I talked about a single mom who lost a tremendous amount of weight and now trains other people to do the same? All of the challenges you've managed to overcome are a vital part of your journey. Own them. This is a powerful tool to bond with your audience.

For example, in the trailer for my public speaking course, I admitted to my audience that I used to be deathly afraid of presenting. In fact, on one occasion, I even ran away from the stage, leaving 100 of my fellow students in a state of shock. Mentioning this story in the trailer gives potential students an instant connection to me. Those who have felt that fear immediately know I understand their struggle. I used to share the same pain point as them, but I found a way to overcome it. Now, I was going to show them how to overcome it too.

You may be thinking that sharing something like that will make you look weak. Nope. When you combine vulnerability with credibility, you create a beautiful cocktail of authentic power. In this particular trailer after I shared my struggles I added B-roll footage of me presenting on massive international stages. All of this solidified my image as an expert in the viewer's mind. An overcomer! For instance, my fellow Mindvalley Author, Jim Kwik, shares very openly in his online course that he was the "boy with a broken brain." It makes him relatable, and today, Jim helps millions of people improve their memories.

By honestly talking about my past and current challenges, I help create an instant trust and bond that makes people want to learn more. Are there any opportunities for you to embrace vulnerability? Can you include some self-deprecating humor, or share a fun fact or story about yourself that authentically shows your human side? If that's the case, even if that story isn't connected to the course topic, you'll appear more likable and relatable to your viewers.

THE THIRD ELEMENT: CLEAR BENEFITS

Make sure to list all the benefits your students will get as a result of taking your course. When you speak about positive outcomes, people can vividly imagine the changes they will be able to make in their own lives. It fires them up and gets them more excited about diving into your videos. Fortunately, this part is simple since we've already done most of the work in *Your Niche & Audience Identification* part of this book. Think back to the major benefits your customer avatar will get, and deliver those key takeaways compellingly.

THE FOURTH AND FIFTH ELEMENTS: CALL TO ACTION (CTA) AND MONEY-BACK GUARANTEE

Never assume that just because someone likes your trailer they will then make a buying decision. People often need an extra push. That's why you should always tell them exactly what you want them to do next. When you watch my trailers you'll see I almost always say something along the lines of: "Go ahead and enroll in this course right now. After all, someday and tomorrow never come. Besides, there's a 30-day, money-back, hassle-free guarantee so you can change your mind anytime. Enroll today. I'm excited to see you on the other side!"

By stating the **call to action (CTA)** and including a clear **money-back guarantee**, you have a huge impact on what your prospects are focusing on. Instead of leaving them to think about it and come back later, you nudge them to enroll in your course right away: "Jimmy makes some good points. There is no risk. I can get my money back for 30 days. Hmmm, why not? Hold on, where's my credit card?" Inserting a confident call to action in your video, combined with a money-back guarantee, will unquestionably increase your conversion rates.

You can see some examples of trailers that have worked exceptionally well for me on the resources page: **www.jimmynaraine.com/coursecreationresources**

THINGS TO REMEMBER

- The purpose of a promo video is to grab attention and showcase all the reasons why your audience needs to enroll in your course.

- Learn from successful promotional videos, but don't be afraid to experiment with unique ideas.

- Create a captivating trailer to grab attention and increase enrollments.

- Start with an emotional hook point, addressing the viewer's pain points.

- Combine credibility and vulnerability to build trust and connection.

- Emphasize clear benefits and outcomes of the course.

- Use a powerful call to action (CTA) and offer a money-back guarantee.

CHAPTER 12

ESSENTIAL INGREDIENTS OF COMPELLING CONTENT

Have you ever started reading a book so enthralling that you just couldn't put it down? Have you ever watched a movie or a speech that made you forget about reality? Perhaps it was so emotional and intellectually engaging that time stopped and you forgot where you were. Achieving this state in viewers is the holy grail of any creator. The billion-dollar question is: What makes some content so captivating and engaging that people find it irresistible? Most importantly, what can you do to design your courses so they trigger a similar response?

Let's talk about various ingredients of compelling online course content. You don't have to implement all of them, but at least some combination of the following building blocks will make it more likely your students will stay engaged:

1. Authentic personal experiences.
2. Case studies and references.
3. Clear action steps & exercises.
4. Guest lectures.
5. Giving secrets away.
6. Bonus lectures and frequent updates.

Let's discuss these elements in more detail.

AUTHENTIC PERSONAL EXPERIENCES

Sharing your personal experiences helps you to bond with your audience. This is especially true when some of your stories have an element of vulnerability. Also, talking about real examples from your own life makes concepts easier to understand and relate to. On top of that, it shows your audience that you have experience in what you are discussing. It allows them to see that you didn't merely regurgitate a bunch of ideas found online in hopes of making a quick buck. You walk your talk.

For example, when I was shooting my travel hacking course, I did it while traveling to distant and exotic locations. The credibility that came from shooting in various settings, combined with relevant personal stories, made it clear that I was qualified to teach about world travel.

CASE STUDIES AND REFERENCES

Case studies are critical for two reasons. First of all, they give your content more credibility. Secondly, they make it easier for people to understand the real-life applications of what you teach. I also believe in referencing various sources, whether books, scientific research, quoting other thought leaders, etc. Make sure that whenever you reference something you give original authors the credit they deserve.

When I share content with my audience, whether on a stage, during live interviews, or in my courses, I like to give examples from the fascinating books I've read. It is a true win-win. It makes my overall content more compelling and credible and sends valuable traffic towards the authors I'm referencing.

For instance, recently I created bonus videos sharing what I'd learned while conversing with Remi Adeleke, a former Navy Seal. I also mentioned some key takeaways from my experience of being a speaker at Bruce Lipton's (a well-known biologist) seminar. In other videos, I talked about takeaways from my deep dive with renowned author Steven Pressfield, and an interview I did with Ollie Ollerton, the star of the British TV show *SAS: Who Dares Wins*. On one hand, the lessons I conveyed to my audience were extremely valuable for them. On the other hand, by sharing these examples I also promoted the works of the aforementioned individuals. I also benefited from **the "rub-off" effect**. Even though I'd solely focused on delivering value in my videos, many members of my audience were likely thinking: "Hmm, Jimmy gets to converse with all those public figures. They're clearly taking him seriously. Maybe I should, too." This side effect gives an extra boost to my credibility in the eyes of my audience.

Chances are, after reading the previous paragraph you got curious. Perhaps you even Googled the conversations I had with Remi, Bruce, Steven, and Ollie. The good news is that you don't need to personally know or speak to famous people in order to create a win-win. You can benefit from the "rub-off" effect simply by referencing high-profile individuals in your content, giving the credit where it's due.

CLEAR ACTION STEPS & EXERCISES

No matter what your course is about, I'm sure you'll agree with the following statement: Consuming great content without taking any action is a form of procrastination. As an instructor, you have to make it easy for your students to implement what you are teaching. Don't leave them to take action on their own; many folks never get around to it.. They may think: "I'll implement all the advice once I complete the course." You need to propel them throughout the course to take specific action steps along the way. This is precisely why I am doing my best to give you various action steps in this book. I don't want you to merely read this book's advice, I want you to live and breathe it.

For example, I took a book-writing course hosted by Scribe Media (which I highly recommend). Tucker Max, Scribe's founder and a multiple *New York Times* bestselling author, led the session. What I liked most was that each participant received a Google sheet with various exercises and questions to answer. Tucker took us through every single activity and made us take action right away. This approach was simple yet powerful.

When you design your practice activities, don't overcomplicate things. Make them simple enough to ensure that people follow through. It could be as simple as asking them to answer a question, or giving them a hands-on task that takes only 60 seconds to complete. The objective is to get your students going and help them to build momentum. Gradually, as they progress through the course, you can increase the difficulty of each task.

To give you an example, in some of my confidence-building courses I propel viewers to push out of their comfort zone through various challenges. I make the first task relatively easy so that anyone can complete it. However, towards the end of the course, I ask the participants to do something significantly more uncomfortable.

Many people find this approach very valuable. I don't know what your subject matter is, but I'm sure that you can think of progressive action steps to guide your viewers toward their goal.

GUEST LECTURES

Involving **guest lecturers** can be a game changer, especially if you have access to someone who has relevant knowledge that is slightly different from your content. So how do you find a guest lecturer? The easiest way is to tap into your network. As well, reach out to people with a solid track record who seem like a good match. The incentives you can offer depend on factors such as:

- The depth of their contribution (short video vs. full section vs. a majority of the course).
- Their status, reach, and experience.
- Your personal dynamic with them.

How you incentivize them depends on your circumstances. In some cases, they may agree to a free contribution for the exposure. However, if their contribution is significant or the person is well known in the industry, you could offer them a one-off cash payment or even a percentage of the profit.

GIVE YOUR SECRETS AWAY

To this day, I meet people who have the mistaken idea that keeping their best secrets hidden is the way to operate. In reality, this approach is a sure path to failure. We live in a world where knowledge is freely available. Virtually anything you want to learn can be Googled for free. As I said at the beginning of this book, the information age is dead. We've already moved into the "personal transformation" economy. When people buy your course, they aren't merely paying for your knowledge. They're paying for your expert guidance. To stand out, you have to continually exceed expectations. This means you have to get comfortable with giving away your best secrets.

Some people worry that if they share their "life-changing" strategies, they won't get consulting or coaching clients. WRONG. Dead wrong. Once again, when people pay you for your time, it's not about information. It's about much more than that. In fact, by revealing your best-kept secrets, you show your potential clients precisely why they should choose you.

People want to work with you because they want to have direct access to personalized guidance. Instead of holding back, you should reveal all your best tools and strategies in your courses. If you do this, people will want to work with you even more.

I'm an advocate for laying everything out there based not only on my personal experiences but also those of my friends and colleagues. Even though I've published thousands of videos that reveal all my key lessons and insights, I keep getting approached by high-profile clients who are keen to pay top dollar for consulting, coaching, or corporate training. By exceeding your audience's expectations, you will stand out from your competition. Your course will serve as living proof that you are the leading expert in your field, which will draw in potential clients and business partners.

BONUS LECTURES AND FREQUENT UPDATES

Creating a course is not a one-and-done affair. If you want to be successful in the online space you need to keep serving your clients and continually update your courses. This includes checking for any errors, updating outdated material, creating bonuses requested by your students, etc. This can be time-consuming, but I recommend that you complete a proper audit of your classes at least once per year to ensure you maintain top-notch quality. When you do that you'll exceed your audience's expectations. Here's the secret though. You don't need to create bonus content in real-time. In fact, I recommend that during the main video shoot, in addition to your core content, you also come up with several extra videos. Those lectures don't have to be inextricably connected to the core subject of the course. Still, they should be relevant enough to provide immense value to your audience. Instead of releasing those content pieces right away, post them several months after your publish date. This approach has two significant benefits. First of all, it increases the perceived value of your course, since everyone loves free bonuses. Secondly, it eliminates the possibility of you procrastinating, as you will create everything for your course right from the start, and then it's ready to be uploaded when the time is right.

THINGS TO REMEMBER

- Share authentic personal experiences to build trust and help your audience relate to you.

- Use case studies and references to establish credibility and demonstrate real-life applications.

- Provide clear action steps and exercises to facilitate implementation and build momentum.

- Consider incorporating guest lectures to diversify your content and add unique perspectives.

- Give away your best secrets to significantly exceed expectations.

- Offer bonus lectures and regularly update your courses to maintain high quality and prove to your audience that you genuinely care.

- Create simple, progressive practice activities to guide students toward their goals.

- Use the "rub-off" effect by referencing high-profile individuals, always giving credit where it's due.

CHAPTER 13

CRUCIAL CONTENT CREATION RULES

So far you've learned about the vital ingredients of a successful online course, from understanding the building blocks of a landing page and your course structure, to creating compelling content pieces. In this chapter, we will touch on some other, equally important, rules and strategies to keep in mind when building your course.

When designing your online course content, don't make it your first goal to generate income. Instead, focus on providing immense amounts of value; the money will come. Actually, money isn't real. It's just a medium of exchange. It's a piece of cotton fiber or a string of digits we assign value to. When you sell a course, you offer something of value that people are willing to pay for. VALUE is the key word here. At every step along the way, keep asking yourself:

- How can I radically exceed expectations and trigger massive transformation for my customers?
- How can I get my students to implement what I'm teaching to get instant results?

You see, the key to making money is actually not constantly obsessing over making money. Focusing solely on generating revenue is a bit like being a dog chasing its tail. You end up obsessing about that one thing and forget that the only thing that justifies your revenue is becoming a true catalyst for your audience's transformation. You can't overly focus on the outcome (money) at the expense of your mindset and actions that can get you that outcome. It's wiser to obsess over creating immense value for your audience, knowing deep inside that it will inevitably lead to all types of rewards.

Here's a good metaphor. If you want to build muscle, you have to do some type of training. You hit the gym, lift weights, break the microfilaments in your muscle tissue, and propel them to grow bigger and stronger. You can't merely command your muscles to grow. It is the hard work that comes first. You cannot simply exclaim: "Hey muscles, can you please grow so I can lift that heavy kettlebell?" Unfortunately, this is the way most people approach generating money through online education. They focus on the money, disregarding the value creation.

Some aspiring course creators reluctantly confess: "I don't want to invest too much time and effort if I have no guarantee that anyone will buy my course." This mindset will get you nowhere in the online teaching business. Does it mean you shouldn't publish concise courses? Absolutely not. In fact, I encourage people to start with a shorter product AS LONG as it's packed with value. People who publish half-baked lectures in the hope of "getting that lambo" don't last long. What's more, you must remember that each piece of content you publish impacts your online brand. Warren Buffet famously said: "It takes 20 years to build a reputation and five minutes to ruin it." Never forget that. Put your heart into the process and always focus on creating a lasting transformation for your audience.

EACH VIDEO "SELLS" THE NEXT ONE

If someone enrolls in your course, they must be fully invested, correct? Negative. People often make rapid buying decisions influenced by a mixture of factors, including:

- Your title, subtitle, and course image.
- How well you address their pain points on the landing page.
- Availability of time-sensitive discounts.
- Promotional videos.
- Social proof (reviews, testimonials, and the number of students enrolled).
- Your overall credibility as an author.
- Free preview videos.
- Special bonuses.

It's not uncommon for people to buy well-positioned courses on an impulse. In some cases, they don't even browse any lectures right away but simply want the access for later. Finally, they start watching your videos, they are subconsciously (and often consciously) trying to determine whether to proceed further. After all, time is their most valuable resource. You need to make sure that you "hook" your viewers from the start and that you keep them hooked all the way through to the end. In essence, each video should make them want to watch the next one.

Does the following sound familiar?

You have two hours to relax in the evening, so you settle in to watch *Game of Thrones*. Nine hours later, as the sun is coming up, you start squinting in dramatic realization that you've been glued to the screen all night long. It's incredible how the best screenwriters manage to keep people engaged. One of their strategies is to increase the level of suspense at the end of each episode. When this happens, you feel like it's almost impossible to return to your regular life without finding out what happens next. This pattern repeats itself over and over again, keeping us hooked through to the end.

While learning from online classes is different from watching an action-packed television series, some parallels do exist. When building your content, make sure it's captivating from the very beginning. Avoid lengthy introductions, make your delivery charismatic, share engaging stories, provide interesting examples, and be authentic. Also, focus on your customer's pain points and deep desires. Whenever you can, try to "hype-up" upcoming lectures by triggering curiosity towards the end of each video. Remember, each video "sells" the next one.

WHAT'S IN IT FOR THEM

In your videos you may want to share various stories and anecdotes from your own life. This allows you to cultivate a stronger bond with your audience, but make sure you stick to the main topic of your course. Sometimes aspiring online course creators feel compelled to share as much as possible about themselves, even if it means going radically off-topic. Participants are taking your course because they want to learn something new, overcome a challenge, or find a solution to a pain point. They are NOT taking your class to get to know you. The bottom line is this. Your viewers will only care about your anecdotes as long as they serve a clear educational or inspirational purpose.

During your production process, remind yourself that your customers' most important question is: "What's in it for me?" When I did training with Tucker Max, who's sold over five million books, he said something I will never forget. "People are not reading your memoir to learn about your life. They read it to learn about theirs." This golden rule applies to any form of content creation, including producing online courses.

THINGS TO REMEMBER

- Prioritize value over income. Focus on delivering high-quality, transformational content that exceeds your students' expectations rather than obsessing over revenue.

- Never shy away from putting in the work if you want to stand out. Short courses are fine as long as you pack them with value.

- Keep students engaged by making each video captivating. Ensure that each lecture "sells" the next one, using techniques like suspense, storytelling, and addressing pain points.

- Remember that it's not about you but the value you create for your audience. Share stories and anecdotes only when they serve an educational or inspirational purpose.

- Remember that your students keep asking themselves: "What's in it for me?" Always focus on helping them learn, overcome challenges, and find solutions to their pain points.

CHAPTER 14

STEP-BY-STEP CURRICULUM CREATION FORMULA

Even with clear objectives, a precise roadmap, and vast knowledge of your topic, it's easy to fall into a trap similar to writer's block. Staring at a blank page can feel paralyzing for anyone, even the most experienced authors. The first draft of anything is always dirty. It's not meant to look great. At least, not yet. Remove the pressure of getting everything just right and trust the process. Once you complete your first draft, you'll be able to polish it. For now, concentrate solely on building the raw material. In the following pages, you will learn the exact steps (within clearly defined phases) to design your course curriculum.

REVERSE-ENGINEER YOUR CURRICULUM

One of the biggest mistakes aspiring course creators make is starting from A and slowly trying to get to Z. It may sound counter-intuitive, but when designing your curriculum, it's much easier to start with an end in mind. In essence, you first define your Z and gradually reverse-engineer the process until you arrive at a fully optimized course curriculum. I will show you a process I've been refining for many years. The feedback on this process from thousands of people who have implemented it is clear—it saves a huge amount of time and eliminates unnecessary confusion and complexity.

These are the six stages in my curriculum design process:

- Stage 1: Start with the key objectives of your target audience.
- Stage 2: Create a list of frequently asked questions (FAQs).
- Stage 3: Embrace the "idea dump."
- Stage 4: Identify main idea clusters.
- Stage 5: Create a list of all course videos.
- Stage 6: Clarify objectives for each section.

In the following pages, I will break down each one of those stages so you learn exactly what to do and how to implement it. Fasten your seatbelts; let's dive in.

STAGE 1: START WITH THE KEY OBJECTIVES OF YOUR TARGET AUDIENCE

This stage should be relatively simple since you've already chosen your course topic, identified your target audience, and brainstormed your distinct angle. Write down your draft course title on a piece of paper, and jot down the specific objectives of your target audience. Close your eyes, imagine yourself in the shoes of your customer avatar and ask yourself: "What are the key objectives I'd love to accomplish after completing this course?" Then, start jotting them down without overthinking. To make this process more clear and powerful, I will be using an example to demonstrate each stage. Below is the list of potential objectives for a course I'll call *Complete Presentation Skills Masterclass*:

- Learn how to overcome the fear of presenting.
- Become a confident speaker.
- Eliminate speech anxiety.
- Enhance communication skills.
- Learn how to design captivating presentations from A to Z.
- Master charismatic and confident body language.
- Become a more powerful leader.
- Become a captivating storyteller in any situation.
- Understand the impact that great video presenting can have on my business.
- Leverage my upgraded presentation skills to excel at business and social interactions

Writing down these objectives is crucial. You can use these ideas on your landing page to attract potential customers. This list will also help you generate ideas for different content pieces.

STAGE 2: CREATE A LIST OF FREQUENTLY ASKED QUESTIONS (FAQS)

Put yourself in your customer avatar's shoes; jot down the most common questions members of your target audience tend to ask. Whenever you can, I encourage you to involve your actual audience (for instance, friends who could identify with your customer avatar) in this process. Let them know that you are creating a course on *Topic X* and ask them which problems pertinent to that subject they'd like to solve. Ask them to share specific topics or questions that immediately pop into their heads. Always make it clear that there are no stupid questions, and that whatever they reveal stays between the two of you.

Straightforward answers to simple questions is precisely what your audience craves. As an expert in your topic, it's easy to assume that everyone already knows the basics. However, this is often not the case. What you consider to be a "no brainer" could feel like rocket science to the majority of people.

I've studied business and psychology for almost two decades. As a result, concepts such as the Hedonic Treadmill, Pareto Principle, Cognitive Biases, Non-Verbal Pacifying Behaviors, The Imposter Syndrome, etc. are deeply embedded in my brain. Sometimes I tend to forget that most people don't know what all those things mean. Taking this into account, whenever I shoot a video, record a live interview, or give a speech, I remind myself to explain those concepts before talking about them. In a nutshell, asking your audience what they want to learn is always a winning strategy.

What if you don't have an existing audience or people in your life that represent your customer avatar? The solution is simple. Tap into the power of social networks. I'm sure some people from your **extended social circle** match your customer avatar. Find them, reach out to them, describe your project, and ask for their input. Remember to address what's in it for them right away. I always do my reach-out in private and offer free course access to anybody willing to give me some honest feedback. Don't be a cheapo, and don't try to sell to the people who help you. Instead, create a win-win scenario for them and you.

Also, become active in **social media groups** that are populated by your target audience. Investigate what questions, issues, and challenges tend to come up. This provides an excellent opportunity to start sharing your knowledge. It also contributes to your online credibility and will draw in new followers.

As a part of your pre-launch, you could host a free, value-packed webinar followed by a Q&A session to pull valuable information directly from your target audience. If this sounds too overwhelming, you could simply schedule a free group coaching session with several people who represent your avatar. Alternatively, you could conduct a series of LIVE videos on your preferred social media platform digging into various topics you consider teaching in your online course. Also, in most cases it may be a good idea to offer audio-only sessions as it makes people more comfortable, and likely to open up. For example, some of the most common questions in our pretend **Complete Presentation Skills Masterclass** course may include the following:

- How do I calm my nerves before public speaking?
- What should I do with my hands when I'm on the stage?
- I'm afraid I'll go blank on stage. Should I memorize my speech?
- What can I do if I start panicking on stage?
- What's the best way to design my presentation?
- Should I always use slides?

Knowing the biggest challenges your target audience struggles with (especially spoken in their own words), gives you a lot of clarity when planning and creating your content.

Finally, as mentioned in the previous part of this book, make sure that you analyze what your competition is doing. Take some time to go through their landing pages, reviews, and even lectures to see how you can over-deliver with your content. Ask yourself: "Is there something that my target audience wants, that the competition is not giving them?" Then plan carefully how to fill that gap to exceed expectations

STAGE 3: EMBRACE THE "IDEA DUMP"

All right, by now, you've outlined your course objectives and determined your audience's frequently asked questions (FAQs). Next, I want you to take a piece of paper and start brainstorming every single content piece that could help you fulfill those objectives. This may sound overwhelming, but here is a surprise. Most (if not all) of the frequently asked questions you wrote down in the previous stage could serve as separate lectures. Am I right? The same thing applies to your course objectives. I bet that some of them could serve as full sections (more about that shortly). Sometimes the answers you are seeking are… right in front of you. After completing stage two, you will undoubtedly have solid lecture ideas that, most importantly, are in tune with what your target audience is looking for!

A big part of your job is already done. However, something tells me that there is more you can give. Take a notepad, and think about every single content piece you could possibly teach within your topic to serve your customer avatar. When I say content, I mean anything and everything that could help your audience: authentic personal experiences, case studies, references, clear action steps, exercises, secrets, maybe even potential guest lectures.

Let's get back to our example of designing a Complete **Presentation Skills Masterclass.** Here is a mixture of draft content pieces that we could write down in our idea dump for this specific course:

- Stories of transformation.
- The physiology behind stage fright.
- Why rejection is hardwired, and why it's an illusion

- The biggest mistakes to avoid when presenting.
- "Emergency" video lecture for those who will present today.
- Action step: film a mock speech.
- The secret to never forgetting the flow.
- Reference a few TED talks.

As you can see, it's a mixture of different types of content. Some of those items are specific, and some of them are broad. It doesn't matter at this stage. It's just the clay you will use later on to "sculpt" an intelligent (and compelling) curriculum. Whenever something comes to mind, jot it down. Don't overanalyze it. Let your creative juices flow without judgment. Ideally, you'll go through this process in several sessions as, over time, you will be getting fresh ideas. I recommend that you keep a little notepad or paper in your pocket at all times (or add notes on your phone and keep them organized in a digital project folder). Be proactive about figuring out new angles for potential educational material.

Whenever you stumble upon something that could benefit the course, document it. Most importantly, don't overestimate the power of your memory, and always make a note about your source to easily give credit where credit is due. There are many people who think that "borrowing" other people's content is acceptable. It is not. It's pure theft (and plagiarism is illegal). I've been a victim of it way too many times, and it's not pleasant. Quoting people, bringing up case studies, etc. is great, but only when you credit the original source.

STAGE 4: IDENTIFY MAIN IDEA CLUSTERS

Go through the list several times, and let it marinate in your head. Then identify the big picture ideas. Ask yourself: If I were doing a live workshop or explaining this topic to a friend, what main ideas would I discuss?

These **idea clusters** will serve as your *sections*. Please remember that none of this has to be perfect, as we are still deep in the draft mode. For now, create draft section titles that represent main course ideas.

For instance, in our sample course, a content piece called "How to stop negative thoughts before you present" could be a great lecture. However, "How to overcome fear" is much broader and could serve as a great section (idea cluster).

Once you have a draft of potential sections, determine what the optimal order might be. For example, if you are teaching an introductory course on basic web design, you wouldn't start with advanced HTML. You would probably begin with an Introduction section to explain the basic concepts and then create a second section about securing a domain name, finding a hosting service, and determining the right theme. The third section could be about different plugins you could use, such as Elementor, with each lecture explaining each one in detail. The fourth section could be about strategies and tools essential to draft a big picture strategy for your website. And you continue on from there.

When you set out to structure your course content, in most cases you want to make sure that idea clusters are in a logical order. Essentially, each section's knowledge supports the next one. You then follow the same rule for the videos within each section. It's just like building a house. You can't start laying the bricks for the walls or install the windows if you don't have a solid foundation built first. However, there are exceptions. For some courses it may be better to create standalone sections and videos. In such a case, each section (or video) can be watched independently of the rest.

Let's get back to our example, ***Complete Presentation Skills Masterclass***. Here are possible section titles arranged in a logical order:

- Section 1: Introduction & Public Speaking Fundamentals.

- Section 2: How to Handle Fear and Present with Confidence.

- Section 3: Learn to Design Your Presentation Flow.

- Section 4: Strategies to Present Like a Winner.

- Section 5: Powerful Body Language in Public Speaking.

- Section 6: The Biggest Public Speaking Mistakes to Avoid.

- Section 7: Answers to Frequently Asked Questions.

What about the number of sections? Well, that depends on your topic and the overall length of the course. I recommend that you imagine giving a live workshop with bathroom breaks in-between the main idea clusters. Envision that you are lecturing your target audience. How would you logically divide all your material into blocks to make everything smooth and digestible?

A rule of thumb is that you should avoid having more than ten videos per section, as too many videos in a section can become tedious or overwhelming for students. If you still end up with more than that, consider splitting the section into two parts. As always, please remember that there are exceptions to almost any rule.

Finally, it bears repeating... Please, don't become a victim of perfectionism. I know you intend to do your absolute best, but always remember that this is just a draft that you can improve later.

STAGE 5: CREATE A LIST OF ALL COURSE VIDEOS

Let's check your progress. So far, you have a draft outline of your course sections in the optimal order. You've also done your idea dump, and have listed your possible content pieces (lectures). Now you are ready to fill each section with the relevant video lectures from your idea dump. You may still feel slightly overwhelmed at this stage, trying to make sense out of all your notes. You may also be second-guessing your ability to pull off such a (only seemingly) big endeavor. This feeling is entirely normal and expected. It means that you care. Again, don't stress about making things perfect; your first draft is meant to be imperfect. In the following pages, I will show you a proven process that makes everything more intuitive, simple, and fun!

For extra clarity in this fifth stage, let's break everything down into specific steps.

Step 1: Write down each one of your draft section titles in bold on separate blocks of paper. For example:

> Paper 1: **Section 1: Introduction & Public Speaking Fundamentals.**
>
> Paper 2: **Section 2: How to Handle Fear and Present with Confidence.**

And so on.

Then, position these blocks on the floor in the correct order, with plenty of space in between them. If you want to see some visual examples visit my resources page: **www.jimmynaraine.com/coursecreationresources**

Step 2: Transfer all items from your content brainstorming list (idea dump from Stage 3) onto separate sticky notes. Each content idea is a potential lecture, but you can also combine two or more content ideas into one lecture. For example, you may combine a piece of knowledge with a personal story and an action step into one lecture (or any other combination). Each lecture requires a draft title.

For instance, in our ***Complete Presentation Skills Masterclass*** example, we could combine the following content pieces from the idea dump into one lecture:

- Explaining the physiology behind stage fright, and
- Action step: Film a mock speech.

For example, we could call this lecture: "This Powerful Action Step Will Make You Confident" and in it explain to the viewers what happens physiologically when they experience stage fright and how they can overcome it by practicing with mock speeches. Naturally, this is just one out of many possible examples, but I just wanted to illustrate how you can combine various elements from your idea dump.

Step 3: Jot down each one of those potential lectures on separate pieces of paper. To maintain clarity, limit yourself to writing just one draft title on each sticky note. Then position all of them on the floor a meter from the blocks with your draft section titles. The reason we are doing all of this is because having the visual representation of your entire course in front of you will enable you to see how various content pieces connect to form the big picture.

Step 4: Begin with section 1. Look at all your sticky notes and ask yourself: Which of them are relevant for this section? Once you identify them, start positioning those content pieces beneath that section title. There's no need to overthink, as you can keep amending the order until satisfied with the final curriculum.

You may have a massive number of potential lectures. That's good. It gives you more raw material to play with. Don't feel the pressure to use every single one of them in the course. Pick only the topics that are relevant and feel right in the end.

Step 5: Repeat the same process for each subsequent section. If you feel like adding a new topic idea you hadn't thought about before, go for it. You may even realize at some point that some draft lectures can be merged into one. That's fine too.

The process I just described may require a couple of hours. In fact, it's wise to take a break, get a good night's sleep, and revisit everything the next day with a fresh perspective. Keep refining your course outline using sticky notes until you feel you have a strong organization. Then, type your structured outline into your laptop and keep tweaking details until you're 95% satisfied (chasing perfection often causes procrastination and paralysis). If you put in the effort, you'll get to the point of looking at your course curriculum with childlike excitement, thinking: "This is so good. People will love it."

Feel free to "bend" my strategy based on your situation. Also, because you may want to make changes to your course content later, **never** mention the lecture number in your videos. You want the flexibility to move things around even once the course is published (as I've done so many times). Also, you may want to document your progress by clicking a photo of your papers from time to time. The last thing you want is your pet chewing away your hard work or a breeze blowing everything into chaos.

STAGE 6: CLARIFY OBJECTIVES FOR EACH SECTION

You've identified the main goals of the course. You've prepared the list of all the vital sections in optimal order. Now, I want you to take this a step further and figure out the objectives for each section. I want you to literally repeat stage 1, but for every single section. This list will be valuable when you create your section introduction videos, as it will help you to entice your students to keep going through the course. Always remember that in order to maximize your course completion rate, you must continuously get your students excited about the content that lies ahead.

Finally, please remember that content creation can be much more than writing down your notes and then presenting them. Open your mind, try various approaches, and see what unleashes your creative juices.

I often get inspired when spending time in nature, exercising, or while driving. Whenever I get an exciting idea, I do my best to capitalize on it. Instead of missing out on the opportunity to capture something valuable, my notepad is always ready. Sometimes, I randomly pull out my phone and record audio notes about what I'm pondering. The key here is to simply capture your thoughts with zero pressure on evaluating the usefulness of the ideas. It's about honoring the creative state without self-judgment.

Later on, I either listen to my notes and jot down the vital points, or I use an AI transcription software such as otter.ai to effortlessly produce a full text. This approach has been working exceptionally well for me. It allows me to use my daily experiences as a positive trigger to create original content. I don't know your personal circumstances, but I'm sure that you can use those tools to spice up your content generation process too.

THINGS TO REMEMBER

- Reverse-engineer your curriculum: Start with your end goals in mind and work backwards to create an intelligent course flow.
- Follow my proven 6-stage curriculum design process.
- Visualize yourself as your target customer and list the key objectives they crave.

- Compile a list of FAQs: Involve your actual audience to identify common questions and concerns.

- Leverage social networks and communities and gather insights by engaging with your audience.

- Embrace the "Idea Dump": Brainstorm all possible content pieces that could help fulfill your course's objectives, drawing from FAQs, personal experiences, case studies, and more.

- Organize content visually: Write draft section titles on separate blocks of paper and transfer content ideas onto sticky notes, then arrange them logically, creating a visual map of your course structure.

- Focus on progress rather than (toxic) perfectionism. Refine your course outline until it's 95% satisfactory, remembering you can make adjustments even after the course is published.

- Utilize tools like notepads, voice recording, or AI transcription software to enhance your content generation process and draw inspiration from daily experiences.

PART 4

PRODUCE TOP-QUALITY COURSES ON ANY BUDGET

It's my first time recording in a professional studio. I was so anxious before coming here that I practiced everything ten times over the weekend. My heart pounds in my chest, my palms are sweating, and I just hope that nobody will notice how nervous I am.

Powerful studio lights make my eyes squint, but I assume that this is only a part of the process. I'm about to begin my presentation, and for some reason, my brain feels empty.

"Get your shit together, man," I whisper to myself. I try to rationalize that what I'm experiencing now is just excitement. Suddenly, I hear: "Action!" and begin to speak.

Less than 20 seconds into the video, and I make a mistake. Delete. Start over. Such an amateur!

I've paid for just two hours of studio time. If I don't get into the flow state right away, I'm not going to finish even half of the course—bye-bye to my project. I ask for a 60-second break, close my eyes, and take a few deep breaths. I remind myself of the vision I've created so vividly in my mind. I remind myself that this video shooting is not just about me; it's about all the people I can help overcome anxiety and low self-esteem. I'm not trying to be a fucking guru; I just want to be a humble messenger.

I recalibrate and start again.

This time I feel it. It seems like the words are flowing out by themselves. I keep going at a decent pace. Two hours later, I hear something that ends up changing my entire life: "The way you present is very captivating, you know? What if we forget that cash payment? Why don't we start working together instead?"

Even now, looking back at that first shooting session makes me quite emotional. Over the years, I've gotten used to the idea that I share video content with people worldwide. I often forget that the dream life I usually take for granted was so close to not happening. How fortunate I am that things worked out the way they did. Where would I be right now if those two hours in the studio were all I'd ever had?

I want you to be in my shoes soon too, looking back at your first shoot, seeing how far you've come and wondering, *What if I'd never given that a try?*

Let's Get Your Course Produced!

In this part of **Course Creation Simplified** I'll discuss the options you have to film your videos. As I promised you when we started, you don't need money bulging out of your pockets to shoot a high-quality course. You have many different options, some of which can be done on an almost non-existent budget. I will also address one of the most common questions I receive: "Jimmy, I'm not a talented public speaker. How do I manage my fear and confidently present so people actually watch my videos?"

I'll answer that question and many more. I hope that you are excited. Let's go!

CHAPTER 15

FILMING OPTIONS FOR ANY BUDGET

There are basically five methods to choose from for filming your course. In the following pages, we'll discuss each one of them in more detail to give you all the clarity you need:

1. Pay a professional.
2. Collaborate with percentage share.
3. Collaborate with value exchange.
4. 100% DIY (do it yourself).
5. Hybrid DIY.

There's also a sixth way of producing a course, which is by using primarily screencasts. We'll also take a look at that option.

PAY A PROFESSIONAL

This approach is straightforward but certainly requires some financial investment on your part. Not everyone can afford this option. However, if you live in a country where involving a professional without breaking the bank is possible, I suggest you go for it. There is a common misconception that hiring a pro is reserved solely for the rich. Many people tell me: "Jimmy, I don't have thousands of dollars lying around." Sure, some places in the world lack affordable options. However, more often than not, this isn't the case.

Moreover, most people overestimate the time it will take to film their videos and thus the cost. For instance, let's assume that you live in an expensive country, and renting a professional studio together with a camera operator costs a hefty $240 an hour. This may seem like a barrier if you overestimate the time required. How many hours do you actually need to film your (let's say 90-minute) video course? Is it 8 hours, 12 hours, or perhaps even 15 hours? Nope. If you follow my advice, and take your preparation very seriously, it is possible for you to finish in three hours. Suddenly, it's no longer a whopping $1920 dollars for 8 hours or $2880 for 12 hours, but only $720 to get your ENTIRE online course filmed - a course that if designed and executed properly, will keep serving your audience (and you) for many years to come. Naturally, this is just an example, but you see my point. Most people dramatically OVERestimate production costs. Besides, I picked quite an extreme example, as depending on where you are in the world, you can find professionals who charge as little as $12 an hour.

Here's a really out-of-the-box strategy. I know people who plan their holidays in lower-cost countries while fitting in their filming, which is especially clever if you aim to create a lot of video in a short period. For example, let's say that you live in Los Angeles where a studio package will cost you $200 an hour and you plan to shoot 20 hours in total to batch-create course/social media videos for the entire year. Instead of spending a staggering $4,000 in LA, you could go on a two-week holiday to Southeast Asia or Latin America, where studio costs will be just a fraction of the cost in LA. The kicker is that in some cases the savings from this type of geo-arbitrage will basically pay for your entire holiday. This is lifestyle hacking at its best.

What about editing? That's even easier because you can take advantage of **geo-arbitrage** without leaving your house. You can make your money go further by hiring people in lower-cost countries. For instance, you can split filming and editing between different people. You shoot all videos with a local provider, but outsource all editing online. You essentially get the same result for less by hiring a video editor in a developing country who will do a great job for $10 to $15 an hour (and be very satisfied with their rate). While there are different platforms you could leverage to find talent, I like to use Upwork.com. It's reliable, straightforward to navigate through, has a massive pool of talent with verified client reviews, and allows you to use multiple filters to find the best candidates. Upwork also handles safe payments with escrow, and allows you to set various contract types with weekly time limits, time-sheet tracking, and the like.

COLLABORATE WITH PERCENTAGE SHARE

This is how I started, even though it wasn't my initial plan. The collaboration happened organically, and sometimes when life gives you cues, it's wise to follow them. Over the years, many people have been telling me that filming courses is easy for me because I have a video crew. Whenever I hear the "easy" part, I just chuckle to myself. Many also claim that they can't do what I do because they don't have a lot of money. What they don't consider is that, in life, there are different shades of gray. Just because you don't have an essential ingredient doesn't mean you should give up. You can be extremely creative if your "why" is compelling enough (hence, we devoted so much time to defining it earlier in the book).

The truth is that I have never had to pay my video crew. The deal I made with them was straightforward. I gave up a percentage of my online course profit in exchange for their on-going help. How did I know that my courses would be successful? I didn't. However, I was also honest and transparent with them. It was a bet that we decided to take on each other. Worst-case scenario, we would spend a week working on a product that wouldn't earn us a lot of money. Best-case scenario, we'd start paving our way to dominating the market.

You may be wondering: "What's the point of giving away the percentage of your profit if you can just pay someone a flat service fee and keep 100% of earnings?"

Fair question. And I understand where this doubt is coming from. In my case, I got access to a fantastic video crew that was quickly climbing the ranks in the video production industry. Moreover, I could clearly see that they were entirely devoted to our new mission. Initially, we made a deal for just one course. However, we ended up exploring the world together for many years. What I got for the percentage I shared wasn't just a bunch of videos. I got a loyal team.

Look, this approach is not for everyone. In fact, now I mostly pay various professionals and retain all my percentage. However, I'm here to show you possible options so you can make an informed decision. There are pros and cons to contemplate with every option. Ultimately, it depends on your circumstances and who you are planning to partner with. I recommend that you only consider percentage partnerships if you trust the other party and have a shared vision.

Before deciding to go for it, make sure that you discuss all the essential details. My approach before making any business deal is to analyze potential scenarios. You need to make sure that everyone involved is on the same page. Ask: "What do we do if X or Y happens?" Taking care to nail down the details can prevent a lot of drama and potentially risky situations. Also, being meticulous when you formulate your partnership is not a sign of mistrust. On the contrary, it shows you are a professional and that you want to make sure you are both happy with the arrangement over the long term.

It never ceases to amaze me when people make long-term business commitments without spending a mere hour to discuss the details. You always need to remember that everyone can be positive, reliable, and willing to collaborate to the highest standard in the short-term. But it's important to define clear expectations and establish a game plan for the future. Otherwise, it's kind of like getting married to someone without having even one conversation about building a family. When you partner with others to create a course be sure to define the:

- Responsibilities of each party.
- Exact profit share for each party.
- Solutions if <insert potential scenarios>.
- Process for making future decisions.

Partnerships with equity or profit share can be very powerful, but always do your homework and address everything that could later trigger potential complications. It's better to have a few uncomfortable conversations early on to save yourself from thorny issues going forward. Trust me, I learned all of this the hard way. On some occasions in the past I failed to implement my own advice and I paid for it.

You also may be wondering how to split your percentages. I can't give you one straight answer there, as it depends on too many variables. For instance, for projects involving just some studio time/post-production, I've shared only a small percentage of my profit. However, whenever we traveled across the world together with my crew (and they covered their own expenses), the split has been closer to an equal partnership. Having said that, I've always retained the majority share as the face of the brand and the main content driver.

Finally, if you are wondering about payment technicalities, I have some good news. Major course platforms offer automatic payment shares in their dashboards. Each team member automatically gets their share of the profit deposited to their PayPal account or via Stripe.

COLLABORATE WITH VALUE EXCHANGE

Some people prefer to initiate a value exchange partnership. This is a system as old as time. While this may be something that most people wouldn't go for, in some cases it's an excellent strategy. For instance, if someone you know has the skills and the time to help you with video production, and there's something you could do for them in return, perfect! You may be on your way to a win-win partnership by trading services instead of money. As I suggested in my previous point, always make sure that you make the expectations and responsibilities crystal clear to avoid future misunderstandings.

100% DIY

Frankly, the only time I was doing everything by myself was when I started my YouTube channel a decade ago. Later on, I realized that to level up I needed to work as part of a team. There's always a limit to how much you can accomplish by yourself. However, if you want to spend as little money as possible and genuinely like the idea of learning basic filming and editing skills—great! You can surely build an entire course by yourself. It's not that difficult. In fact, it's easier than ever to create an online course.

When I was getting started, the technology wasn't that advanced. Nowadays, you can film a high-quality class with a decent smartphone and a $30 microphone. Editing software is cheaper than ever, but if you're on a shoestring budget, you can also use a free trial version to polish your videos. It's truly remarkable what's possible when you open your mind to find solutions instead of problems.

Let me share a real-life example that's close to my heart. After my initial success with producing online courses, I began to travel and film. I kept sending audio messages to my brother and father, trying to persuade them to give online education a shot. My brother (Adam) was always interested in technical stuff. My father (Roy) is a former medical doctor with many years of experience teaching business English at various companies. Both of them had a lot of value to offer to the world, and I was encouraging them to share it.

At some point, I visited my family in Poland. After many long conversations (some would certainly call it brainwashing) with them, my brother and father decided to take a leap of faith. Adam learned from YouTube how to build a home studio on a tight budget. All the equipment cost him less than $300, and the crazy thing is that they had no other option but to film the course with an iPhone 4!

Guess what happened next? They not only shot the course, but it ended up becoming a bestseller in its category! Since then, Roy and Adam have published more than 20 classes on Udemy.

Delving deep into the specifics of creating a home studio is beyond the scope of this book. There are plenty of YouTube videos that explain the process. Today's advanced technology makes it easy to film a course. It's not crucial to have a pro studio backdrop with a set of lamps. You can film yourself using a basic lavalier microphone (decent ones start at only $30) and a ring lamp that costs roughly the same amount and is easy to use. When selecting your equipment be very careful about any perfectionist tendencies that may cause you to overthink and procrastinate. Set your budget, see what's available, read official reviews, and then give yourself at most a day to make a decision.

If you film outdoors you won't even need to buy a lamp. Just remember that the sunlight should be in front of you. Make sure that you film during the *golden hour*—the pre-sunset window of time when natural light is excellent. Alternatively, you can film outdoors in cloudy weather as clouds diffuse light, making it more even. Also, be careful with filming directly under the intense sun as you will squint your eyes. Of course, you can prevent this from happening by wearing sunglasses, but I did that once, and it was far from ideal. Some people liked it, but I also got feedback that it made me look less trustworthy.

When shooting outdoors the main concern is that you have to be very careful with the **sound**. Based on my experience, the audio quality is the most critical technical factor in shaping user experience. Viewers can't learn anything if they can't hear you clearly. The good news is that microphones are inexpensive. I'm not recommending any specific equipment in this book, as the world of technology keeps changing rapidly, but there are plenty of options. As long as it's not very windy, and you use a clip-on microphone, your sound quality will be more than good enough to safely share your videos with the world. In case you're wondering, I use my phone to film most of my bonus and social media videos. By using my phone I can share them right away. Nobody ever complains about inadequate quality. In fact, did you know that Steven Soderbergh's movie "Unsane" was entirely shot on iPhone 7 Plus?

HYBRID DIY

Finally, if you do not fully resonate with one of the above options, you can combine them in numerous ways. For example, you could pay someone to film you and then do a value exchange with a video editor. Or, you could create your own home video set-up for filming and hire an editor. The options are endless. Think outside the box, be passionate, and go for whatever feels right based on your circumstances. Also, remember that the worst thing you can do is to become paralyzed by overthinking.

SCREENCAST VS. TALKING HEAD VIDEO

Should you always show your face in front of the camera, or is it fine to produce a screencast (also called a screenshare)? This dilemma is a common one, but I will make it simple for you. If you're creating a technical course (all types of programming, graphic design, video editing, etc.), it makes perfect sense to primarily record your screen. After all, it's necessary to visually showcase all the relevant steps in the learning process.

Having said that, even if you're relying primarily on screencasts and slides, I believe that it's essential to reveal your face from time to time. This one simple move can make a difference between selling a trickle of your courses and achieving some level of success. The reason is that people need to trust you to engage in your content thoroughly. It's hard to believe someone if you never see them on screen.

Have you ever received a cold call by a telemarketer with a robotic voice? What was your gut reaction? Probably an immediate: Not interested. Right? What if you're approached in-person by a very charismatic professional who smiles, addresses your silent objections, and speaks your language in a non-pushy manner? Chances are, you might give them at least some of your attention.

As an instructor, you need to do everything in your power to establish trust with your customer. Put yourself in their place. Would you choose a product created by someone who never shows their face? You might even think they have something to hide. Whether that's true or not is irrelevant, since their perception becomes reality.

Now that you see why this is so important, let's speak about the "how." If you're creating a very technical course, keep the bulk of your lectures as a screencast. However, when you are addressing your potential students in the trailer and in the section introductions where you discuss the lesson objectives, show your face. The same goes for the conclusion video, where it makes perfect sense to speak directly to the camera.

Is it possible to create a course in which you never speak to the camera? Yes, it is. But don't expect stellar results. There are exceptions, of course, but the vast majority of people using this approach will not stand a chance in today's competitive online space.

If your objective is to build a business or personal development course, the approach is very different. I can't imagine having a solid course in this arena if you don't speak directly to the camera. Does that mean you have to be standing in front of the lens in every single video? No, of course not. You can have an array of lectures, from a voice-over with slides to screen captures to animations. However, the *majority* of your videos should feature you speaking directly to the camera, especially if you hope to compete with the many courses available in the marketplace that spotlight a captivating instructor.

YOUR ACTION STEP

Analyze the above options in the context of your circumstances. Commit to a strict deadline for making a decision on how to proceed. Remember that being 90% sure and confidently moving forward is always better than trying to be 100% sure but be paralyzed with inaction.

Now that you are familiar with various options for producing your course, let's address a challenge that so many aspiring creators struggle with—video presenting.

THINGS TO REMEMBER

- Choose your production option based on budget & requirements: 1. Pro service 2. Collaboration with % share 3. Value exchanges 4. DIY 5. Hybrid.

- Utilize geo-arbitrage by leveraging smaller costs in developing countries.

- Whenever you make a partnership, clarify the terms: Define expectations, responsibilities, profit share, and solutions to possible challenges.

- Most course platforms allow you to automate profit distribution among team members.

- If you struggle with the budget, tap into your network and embrace win-win value exchanges.

- Remember that producing an online course yourself has never been more accessible, with affordable equipment and software options.

- Think outside the box, and consider combining various filming and editing options.

- In business and personal development courses, speak directly to the camera in all (or at least most) lectures. In technical courses show your face at least in intro videos.

- Remember that being 90% sure and confidently moving forward is always better than trying to be 100% sure and paralyzed with inaction.

CHAPTER 16

OVERCOME YOUR FEAR OF PRESENTING

At the end of this part of the book, I will share a process that will enable you to make your content and delivery "bulletproof." However, before I reveal my strategy, let's spend some time talking about the fear of video presenting.

Why do so many people find that little black lens so terrifying? Well, it has to do with our fear of rejection. When you interact with new people in an informal setting, you're aware of the possibility of rejection. However, you also know that the consequences are almost non-existent. If they show little interest in getting to know you, you simply move on with your day. It doesn't wound you because you know that if people don't value you, you shouldn't spend your time with them in the first place.

But when you get on a stage (or in front of the camera), the situation feels very different. You're now in front of a crowd and your mind starts messing with you. If you make a mistake, everyone will witness it. It's no longer just about brief interactions with a few strangers. The stakes are higher. Suddenly you are exposing yourself in front of tens if not hundreds or thousands of people. The pressure is palpable, and you feel the potential consequences of rejection multiply by the number of people in the audience. Especially if you think about this video being online FOREVER.

This fear of rejection is hardwired in our brains because we humans are tribal creatures. Back in the day, if you got rejected by your tribe, it would mean almost certain death. After all, nobody could survive in a hostile environment without community support. Good luck hunting that big animal without backup, let alone building a shelter and defending yourself from a rival tribe. We're still social creatures, and complete social isolation is almost as good as death for the vast majority of people. Even though our lifestyles have changed dramatically since those caveman days, our old wiring still drives us.

What about a video camera then? Well, even though you may be the only one in the room, you are deeply aware that whatever you film and publish might be viewed by a worldwide audience. You feel the pressure to perform at your best. You know very well that nothing gets permanently removed from the web. Once you post something, you need to assume that it may be there forever. The chances are that some people already made a copy, and there is nothing you can do about it.

The vast majority of people suffer from a disease that may not be officially recognized, but it is prevalent across the globe and ruins many lives. The name of this affliction is "I'm not worthy." We all tend to overestimate other people and underestimate ourselves.

One of the reasons for this state of affairs is that we often see others at their best. Nobody goes on Instagram to post photos of themselves at their worst. Nobody updates their Facebook status to tell everyone: "Hey, I'm a lazy bastard. I haven't read a single book in the last six months." Most individuals don't go to social gatherings in their ratty underwear. The thing is, you see just one angle of people you deal with, and usually, it's the best they can give.

On the flip side, you are with yourself 24/7. You know how much shit you've gone through in your life. You are fully aware that you're far from perfect and that you make many mistakes every day. You still vividly remember those moments when you gave up, succumbed to laziness, hurt someone's feelings... The list goes on.

When you compare yourself to other people online, you are essentially comparing everything you know about yourself to the nicely polished image you see of them. This is always a losing game.

Instead of putting others on a pedestal, you need to remind yourself that they are human, just like you. They have their fair share of fears, weaknesses, past fuck-ups, failures, issues, insecurities, traumas. Looking at it in any other way doesn't make any sense. We often don't trust ourselves, but we should. We often envision just the worst-case scenario, but why not also acknowledge all the exciting possibilities?

Naya Rivera said: "Butterflies can't see their wings. They can't see how truly beautiful they are, but everyone else can. People are like that as well."

Good question to ponder is: "So, why would I be afraid of my content being on the web if I can simply do my best and make sure that each video I produce is something I can be proud of?"

In the following pages, I will take you through several **mindset shifts**. If you want to ensure that nothing will stop you from filming your videos, I recommend that you take notes about the ones that you resonate with the most and keep that piece of paper in your pocket while shooting. Whenever self-doubt creeps in, pull it out and remind yourself that you are simply putting limitations on yourself that don't exist.

NOBODY KNOWS HOW ANXIOUS YOU FEEL

It's true. Nobody really knows how unsure, anxious, or scared you feel on the inside. We often assume that people can see right through us, but they can't. It's completely normal that your body will react to stressful situations by shifting its state. That's how we're designed to function. You may feel your palms and forehead sweating, your heart racing. You may also breathe faster and, as a result, feel slightly light-headed. You may think that everyone, including your video viewers, knows exactly what's happening inside your mind and body. You may be convinced that they can see how stressed you are. However, this is simply not the case.

Think about a duck swimming gracefully along the shore. It appears to be moving effortlessly. What you can't see is the dynamic movement of the duck's feet under the surface. Of course, if you're extraordinarily stressed, people may be able to see signs of it to some extent, but it won't happen in most cases, and even if it does, it won't be as bad as it seems.

One time while feeling absolutely terrible I gave a presentation at a global conference in front of a 500+ person audience.. I was sleep deprived, trying to juggle multiple projects, and on top of that, it turned out that there was a tremendous echo in the room. I could hear my own voice reverberating and because of that, I couldn't fully concentrate. In the first minute, I started sweating, knowing that the next 30 minutes would be a real test of my focus. I was certain everyone could sense my near panic. Interestingly, after the keynote, I received tremendously positive feedback and a lot of people agreed that it was the most impactful speech of the conference. Later on, I saw some video clips from that talk, and to my surprise, there was almost no indication of how I'd been feeling inside. Curious? Search for "Jimmy Naraine DNX" on YouTube and see for yourself.

THE CAMERA IS YOUR FRIEND, NOT YOUR ENEMY

Every time you step in front of a lens you have a choice: The camera can be either your friend or your enemy. Rather than putting tremendous pressure on yourself not to make any mistakes, remind yourself that you're in full control of what will be released to the public. Every time you feel stressed, remember that you can always delete the videos (or at least the fragments) you don't like. This may sound simple, but many people crumble in front of a camera, completely forgetting they have all the power.

Whenever I don't feel my best, I purposely joke around and imagine that I'm doing a practice run, that the footage will be deleted. I get playful, exaggerating my voice modulation and certain gestures just for fun. This seemingly-silly strategy helps me loosen up. Paradoxically, the takes I do just for fun are the ones I often end up publishing.

NOBODY CAN RELATE TO "PERFECTION"

Over the years as I've helped content producers create their online courses, I've noticed that in their minds, "more polished" is always better. It seems like everyone is striving for a perfect presentation with just the right words and impeccable body language. Here's the thing, though: Perfection doesn't exist. And if you try to embrace it, you'll risk coming across as stiff and unrelatable.

Have you ever seen one of those cringe-worthy presentations where it was evident that the author had memorized everything? He or she could clearly recall the text word-for-word, with a fake smile and fake laughter at their own jokes. People don't want to watch videos like that, let alone pay for them. We want to learn from *real* people who struggle just like us. What bonds us together is our common humanity. It's certainly much better to make a mistake while being natural and positive than to recite carefully honed text while being stiff and unnatural.

IT'S NOT ABOUT YOU. IT'S ABOUT THEM.

As you get ready to film your videos, you may worry about how your viewers will perceive you. You may think you don't look good enough or don't have enough "charisma." This is important: Always remind yourself that the videos you are making are not about you. They're about helping your customers. It helps to imagine your customer avatar sitting behind the camera as if you're speaking directly to that person.

Look, I'm just like you. Even though I'm now an expert in course creation, I still experience moments of self-doubt. Everything can be going great and then, suddenly, out of nowhere I hit a mental roadblock. While writing this book, for example, I kept wondering: "What if this book doesn't live up to all my expectations?"

That's when I reminded myself that this project is not about me. It's about sharing all the knowledge and experience I've gained over the years to help you on your journey. As long as I focused entirely on that, I was confident you would find value in these pages.

Embrace this approach when you film your videos, and I guarantee that you will grow wings.

THINGS TO REMEMBER

- Fear of presenting is rooted in our deeply ingrained fear of rejection, and tribal instincts.

- The fear of video presenting is heightened due to our awareness that whatever gets published online will be permanent.

- Comparing yourself to others often leads to feelings of unworthiness and anxiety. Alleviate it by recognizing our shared humanity.

- Embrace your imperfections, remembering that they allow you to connect with your audience authentically.

- Remind yourself that others can't see your inner anxieties and that you have complete control over which videos you will keep or delete. Adopt a playful attitude while filming to loosen up and create engaging content.

- Always imagine speaking directly to your customer avatar, doing your absolute best to help them.

CHAPTER 17

HOW TO BE A MORE NATURAL PRESENTER

Now you have the tools to dance with your fears and present your content with more confidence. In this chapter, you will discover specific strategies you can implement right before (and during) your filming sessions to take your confidence and charisma to another level.

CONSCIOUSLY ENGINEER YOUR "FLOW" STATE

Let me ask you a question. What would you do if you were scheduled to participate in some type of competition tomorrow? Would you just go about your day as usual? Or would you take plenty of time to prepare yourself both mentally and physically?

The answer is obvious. When stakes are high, you don't want to leave things to chance. You'd certainly do your best to get yourself into a "winner" state of mind. When approaching a presentation, prepare as you would for a competition, job interview, or business negotiation. On the day of your filming session, do your absolute best to get into an "I'm a winner" state of mind, as it will make it easier for you to create and enter a flow state.

Mihaly Csikszentmihalyi was the first psychologist to recognize the concept of a **flow state**. He described it as *"a state in which people are so involved in an activity that nothing else seems to matter; the experience is so enjoyable that people will continue to do it even at great cost, for the sheer sake of doing it."* Steven Kotler also dove into the idea of flow state in several of his bestselling books. Here's his very thought-provoking take on flow: *"Flow is more than an optimal state of consciousness—one where we feel our best and perform our best—it also appears to be the only practical answer to the question: What is the meaning of life? Flow is what makes life worth living."*

For me, a flow state is the feeling of being absolutely here and now, fully engrossed in the task at hand, and completely forgetting about the external reality. It's as if your ego dissolves and you become whatever you are doing in that moment. Nothing else is on your radar, and nothing else matters. Engineering a flow state during a presentation is one of the most powerful feelings I've experienced. Suddenly, all the disparate pieces connect and the words are flowing through you. There is no need to plan what you will say next and how you will say it. It is just happening, and in some magical way, you almost feel like an observer.

Various factors can trigger your flow state, and different things work for different individuals. It could be a combination of complete concentration, high-stakes, time pressure, clear and compelling goals, complete autonomy over your task, and more.

Never leave your state of mind to chance. Instead, make a conscious effort to approach filming your course like a winner before you even get in front of that lens. Whenever you are about to present, block some time to get yourself into your "winner" state. Since everyone is different, try various things, see what works best, and then double down on those things. As you gain more experience, you will develop a deeper understanding of what makes you tick and you can create a routine that works for you every time you need to be at your best.

Let me share with you what I do before my presentations to increase the probability of getting into a flow state and feeling like a winner.

First, I don't leave my mental attitude to chance. I control my internal dialog, remind myself that I've done this before, focus on my audience and why they need my help. I also remind myself of my true vision and my compelling WHY (discussed in Part 1 of this book).

Second, I warm up my voice and body. I do this by beatboxing, singing, repeatedly saying (or at least attempting to) complex tongue twisters in various languages, and mouth stretching. I also over-modulate my voice, moving from a gentle whisper to speaking extremely loud (always from my diaphragm), and back. This allows me to extend my natural vocal range and enhance the power of my voice.

Finally, if you are especially nervous, I recommend that you strategically stretch your comfort zone before any filming session. The process of expanding your comfort zone reminds me of something I'm a big fan of, and that is taking an ice bath. As you enter the freezing water, your body will be shocked by the cold. The first 30 seconds can be almost unbearable. However, if you stay in, you gradually adjust to that new environment and you may be surprised that after a few minutes you actually start feeling strangely warm (this is not medical advice, so please consult a doctor before trying this).

During your initial filming sessions you will certainly be pushing out of your comfort zone, so why not stretch it in advance in order to make the "freezing water" feel a bit more bearable? You can do this by performing some uncomfortable exercises prior to your sessions. For instance, before you get in front of the camera or enter a studio you could do a live social media video. Or perhaps you could randomly ask groups of strangers for their opinion on something. You could also take things to the next level (and embrace true awkwardness) by casually singing in public, or doing something equally scary. No matter which comfort zone challenge you embark on prior to filming, I guarantee you that it will recalibrate your relationship with fear. As a result, video presenting itself will no longer feel like such a big deal as you will have sufficiently "warmed up."

THE POWER OF USING YOUR BODY

Body language is very important for two reasons. First of all, if used correctly, the way you use your body can communicate trust, comfort, and confidence to your viewers. Second, your physiology has a tremendous impact on your emotional state. Poor body language will deplete your confidence, and can possibly make you feel tired. Here are some important tips on body language fundamentals that will help you become a more natural-looking presenter.

POSTURE

We all have childhood memories of adults nagging us to keep our backs straight, right? Sadly, due to the nature of our modern lifestyle, we've become a generation of slouchers. Guess what? I used to be one of them, and I still struggle with slouching to this day. Fun fact—I was slouching a little bit while writing the previous point. Now it's back on my radar, and I'm writing with impeccable posture (for now).

When you speak in front of the camera, it's important to keep your back straight. I admit this is easier said than done, especially when filming in a seated position. But after practice, good posture has become a habit for me while shooting. Still, in the early days, I had to set reminders on my phone so I wouldn't forget about it.

If you tend to slouch, create a system that helps you improve your posture. Like me, you can set up simple reminders on your phone such as: "maintain confident posture." Every time one of those notifications pop up, imagine that there is a string going through your spine and that someone is gently pulling its end above your head.

OPEN VS. CLOSED POSITION

Whenever you present anything, whether it's in front of a camera, on a stage, or during a team meeting, it's important to maintain an open position with your arms. Don't let your arms become a wall. The psychology behind this is simple. Whenever you cross your arms, it subconsciously communicates certain things that your audience is not likely to respond positively to.

First of all, it shows defensiveness. It sends the message that you are using your arms as a form of a barricade to separate yourself from the people in front of you. It may also suggest that you have something to hide. You may respond that this is rubbish. Of course you have nothing to hide! However, it doesn't matter. Humans are hardwired to make snap judgments. If the subconscious mind of your viewer feels that your nonverbal signals are a sign of dishonesty, you've lost them, whether you're telling the truth or not.

On the other hand, when you open yourself up, you communicate trust. You show your audience that you have nothing to hide. This is another hardwired response because back in the day humans would open their arms up to prove they had no weapons. Essentially, this gesture communicates: "Look, I'm coming in peace. I have nothing to hide."

You may initially find this shift in your body language slightly weird, especially if you tend to close yourself off. Just keep practicing. With enough repetition this open stance will become your second nature.

Now, let's talk about waving your arms around. Even though gesturing with your arms and hands is a powerful nonverbal signal, please don't feel the pressure to constantly do it throughout your entire video. If moving your arms doesn't come naturally, you can just keep them apart by your sides as a default, while maintaining a straight back. Try to play around with gestures, primarily when you are making important points. Above all, work on it gradually, as feeling comfortable in your skin is paramount. Effective gesturing comes most naturally when you really "connect" with your message. Hence, engineering the flow state we previously discussed is essential.

AVOID THIS TRAP AT ALL COST

Touching your face is one of the biggest mistakes you can make while presenting. Even when you legitimately need to scratch your itchy nose or rub your eye, it's likely to send negative signals to your audience. The damage is immediate. The reason is that we are hardwired to associate people touching or rubbing their faces with insincerity.

Have you ever noticed that small kids often cover their mouths when trying to tell a lie? Intuitively they know that not telling the truth is wrong. Hence, the automatic reaction of covering their mouths.

As we grow older, we learn to adapt and try to hide our true intentions. Still, it's common for many adults to touch or scratch their faces when they are either unsure about something or insincere. If you have to rub your eyes or scratch your face, edit it out, or delete the file and start the video from scratch (pun intended:)). Otherwise, people may misinterpret your nonverbal signals as a sign of dishonesty.

DIRECT "EYE CONTACT"

Unlike in regular conversations, when presenting in front of a camera, you want to maintain direct "eye contact" with the viewers 100% of the time. This would of course feel creepy to someone you're talking to in real life, but the rules governing eye contact are different in video presenting. People's attention span is much shorter, and it's significantly harder to keep them engaged. Hence, it is essential that you keep looking directly at the camera. At first this will feel utterly uncomfortable, but with a little bit of practice you will get there. This is also why I recommend dry practice (more about that soon) before an actual filming session so you get used to this new dynamic.

USE VIDEO TO SPEED UP YOUR FEEDBACK LOOP

The best way to learn how to adapt powerful, positive, and confident body language is to practice in front of a camera. Try different things while recording a video and then analyze the results. This exercise may feel uncomfortable at first, but it will give you the most value in the least amount of time. Nobody but you will see those videos, so be bold and maximize your learning potential. Naturally, the topic of confident and charismatic video presenting can be better explained through videos, and to see the free bonuses I prepared for you, visit my resources page: **www.jimmy naraine.com/coursecreationresources**

THINGS TO REMEMBER

- Consciously prepare yourself mentally and physically for video presentations, just like you would for any competition. Create a powerful routine that helps you enter a flow state.

- Your body language communicates trust and confidence to your viewers and impacts your emotional state. Make it powerful.

- Maintain a straight posture during your presentations. If it's challenging, set daily reminders to develop this habit.

- Always keep an open position, as crossing your arms sub-communicates defensiveness and, in some cases, dishonesty.

- Avoid touching your face, as it is often associated with insincerity.

- Maintain direct "eye contact" with the camera 100% of the time.

- Use video to speed up your feedback loop: Practice in front of a camera to adapt powerful, positive, and confident body language. Analyze the results to improve your presentation skills.

CHAPTER 18

FAQS ON FILMING AND PRESENTING

In this bonus chapter I'll answer some of the most common questions I receive in regards to presenting and filming online courses. I will add extra FAQs to my resources page after collecting fresh feedback from my readers, including you. **www.jimmynaraine. com/coursecreationresources**

"SHOULD I USE A TELEPROMPTER?"

People often ask me about using a teleprompter. I've never done it. Why? Because I believe that delivering compelling content is more about being natural rather than aiming for a perfect word-for-word "performance." As I stressed in the first part of this book, the information age is over. Nowadays, people crave clear guidance presented in a captivating way. In my opinion, as long as you are well-prepared and authentic in your delivery, it doesn't matter if you make a little verbal "goof" here and there.

Having said that, I recognize that every situation is different. Suppose you're making a video where you need to quote lots of data, historical facts, etc. In that case, you may consider using a prompter. Still, I'm a big believer in making things organically because your videos will then come across as more genuine. Not only will you be strengthening your skill in thinking on your feet, you'll also become better at recalling vital information when it matters.

Let me share with you another story. My old friend Seph Fontane Pennock and I went to Bali a few years ago for a filming session. He is the founder of www.positivepsychology.com. We'd planned to record some content together. He had a prompter with him and insisted on using it. However, during our first session, he accidentally dropped it and the glass shattered into tiny pieces.

I'll never forget the expression on his face. He looked as if the world had just ended. After several minutes I patted him on the back and said: "This is probably the best thing that's happened to you this year."

Without a prompter, Seph had no choice but to do everything off the cuff. Initially, it was challenging, as with anything in life that is new. When you were learning how to walk or ride a bike, did you succeed after the first attempt? Of course not, everything takes practice. But as with any skill, persistence brings progress. Within several days Seph was killing it in front of the camera and ended up creating fantastic content. That's when he admitted that I was right. Breaking his prompter really had been a blessing in disguise.

"SHOULD I MEMORIZE THE TEXT FOR EACH VIDEO?"

If you want to memorize any presentation or speech, I recommend you do it only when:

- It's a short promotional video where every word counts.
- You're able to memorize it so well that the delivery will seem natural.

Otherwise, don't do it. Personally, I never memorize my presentations, whether it's on video or stage. Instead, I read bullet points before the shoot, do practice runs to warm up, and then just go for it.

I recommend that you create a very clear outline with bullet points for each video. Then make sure that you practice the full run-through several times before recording. This will help you to learn the content well enough that it "flows" freely but not to the point that it sounds too rehearsed or memorized.

"SHOULD I FILM IN ONE GO OR DIVIDE EACH VIDEO INTO PARTS?"

To make things easier for yourself, you can record each bullet point separately and later connect the clips into one lecture. This approach alleviates a lot of pressure because you don't need to think about too many different things at once. Just take it one point at a time.

For example, your goal may be to shoot 20 six-minute videos. Instead of filming each video in one go, you can divide them into four parts each. This way, you just have to film 80 clips that are only 90 seconds each. Now, the thought of filming 80 clips may seem overwhelming. But if you film 15 short clips each day, you'll be done in about a week. Suddenly, filming a course feels more manageable, doesn't it?

"HOW SHOULD I DRESS?"

The most important thing is that you feel comfortable and that your appearance is congruent with your style. Imagine that you were asked to give a workshop for your target audience. How would you dress? Follow the same strategy when you film.

I'm a minimalist. In most business situations, I wear a black t-shirt, or well-fitted shirt, black pants, and black shoes. The exception is when I speak for big corporate clients and at international business conferences where I sometimes wear a button-down shirt with a jacket. However, I rarely go with a full suit & tie combo, as it's not congruent with my style and brand.

In addition to your personal preference, take your target audience into account. For example, if you teach corporate lawyers, it may make sense to stay on the formal side; whereas, if you teach aspiring gardeners or yogis, you may want to keep it more casual (but still maintain your professionalism).

"HOW SHOULD I ADDRESS MY AUDIENCE?"

Many aspiring video presenters overly preoccupy themselves with the specific words they use, sometimes overcompensating with complicated vocabulary. Nobody wants to listen to jargon.

The most important word you should use when speaking to your audience is "YOU." Essentially, the only thing people care about when they watch your courses is whether you can help them. Always ask yourself: "What's in it for them?" and address your audience directly whenever possible.

This is precisely what I do in all of my courses as well as in this book. I could write about course creation in a more formal way, but you would never have made it to this chapter if that were the case.

There's no reason to try to impress anyone with your intellect. It's never about how smart you are, but about the transformation you can create for your students. Drop your ego and always make your content about them.

THINGS TO REMEMBER

- Utilizing a teleprompter may be tempting, but organic delivery feels more genuine and charismatic. As a bonus, it improves your ability to think on your feet.

- Memorizing the entire video script isn't necessary. Instead, use clear outlines with bullet points for more natural presentations.

- Record each bullet point separately and connect the clips later to make the process more manageable and reduce performance anxiety.

- Dress comfortably and ensure your appearance matches your style while considering your target audience's expectations.

- Focus on addressing your audience directly, using "you."

- Always prioritize creating transformation over trying to impress them with jargon.

CHAPTER 19

FILM A "PAJAMA" DRAFT

You now are clear on how you will film and edit your course. You can also see that all of your fears associated with video presenting are just self-imposed limitations. You realize you are capable of more than you thought you were. You also have the tools to get yourself into the "winner's" state before filming, and you know the best strategies for doing your best in front of the camera.

Now let's talk about something that you need to do to create not just a valuable course, but an *outstanding* course. Interestingly, what I'm about to propose is something that most people are not willing to do. However, it can make all the difference (and it's fun too once you get the first step over with).

Before you even start filming the actual content, I want you to create a "pajama" draft for which there are absolutely zero expectations. A pajama draft is essentially a "dirty" draft of your course that you will never show to anyone. Let me share a short story that illustrates why this approach is so powerful.

Several years ago, a friend (I'm not sharing the name for the reasons you will soon discover) asked me if we could do a video interview together. Naturally, I agreed. As we sat in front of the camera, it quickly became clear something was wrong. He began sweating profusely, his hands were visibly shaking, and on top of that, he started stuttering. I knew exactly what was happening as I'd experienced the same symptoms in the past when I was struggling with a low level of self-esteem and anxiety issues. I knew very well that my friend was heavily stressed about speaking in front of the camera and potentially just a few seconds away from a panic attack. Instead of proceeding with the interview, I decided to make it easy for him. Even though I felt perfectly fine and ready for filming, I said something I knew would work to make him feel comfortable:

> "Hey man, I'm not in the zone today. Can we just do this interview for fun as a little practice run? We can do the real show properly tomorrow. For now, we'll just film it, and then delete it right after, OK? In fact, let's just imagine that we had a few beers, go with the flow and see what happens."

By saying what I did I alleviated all the pressure. Suddenly there were no stakes and he didn't have to live up to any unnecessarily high expectations. Also, I made it look like it wasn't about him not being ready. I made it about me. After I said those words, I witnessed a dramatic change in his physiological reactions and body language. Suddenly, a big smile appeared on his face, he stopped fidgeting, and all the stuttering subsided. When we started filming he was a different person.

That episode fascinates me to this day because the only thing that changed was his perception of the situation. Many of us crumble under pressure. However, when you cleverly remove the pressure you can dramatically improve your performance. And you know what? This doesn't just apply to public speaking. This applies to many realms of life.

For example, my good friend Ilya Grad is a three-time world title holder in Thai boxing. I had the pleasure of getting my ass kicked by him in Thailand. Whenever we meet, he repeats the same advice: "To fight at your best, you need to loosen up. Keeping your muscles tight not only lowers your speed but also makes you get tired faster."

His trick to winning is to train very hard but paradoxically stay relaxed during the fight. This is exactly what you need to do when filming your course.

YOUR PAJAMA DRAFT: ESSENTIAL STEPS

First of all, I call it a **pajama draft** because the purpose of making it is to practice. In some cases, my students end up filming the draft videos in their pajamas or very casual sports clothing just to send a clear signal to their brains: *THIS WILL NOT BE SEEN BY ANYONE!*

In other words, you know that even if your filming session happens to go amazingly well, you cannot possibly use those files because your appearance is completely unprofessional. This eliminates all the pressure. Suddenly, you are just having fun and forgetting about a perfect outcome.

Now, let's walk through the steps to filming your pajama draft.

Step 1

Look at your course curriculum. Focus on the content for the first video. Write down the title on a piece of paper together with all your notes for that particular video.

Step 2

Think about the flow of the video and jot it down in the form of bullet points. Ask yourself: "What do I want to say? In what order do I want to say it?" For example, if I'm making a video about confident body language, my bullet points may look like this:

- Introduction: Hope you're doing well & why positive body language is so powerful.

- First tip: Keep an open position (creates trust, makes you look more positive).

- Second tip: Don't slouch (slouching projects low energy and lack of confidence).

- Third tip: Direct eye contact (only confident people do it, practice daily, if panicking look at forehead).

- Conclusion: Thanks for watching (make sure to practice, see you in the next video).

Step 3

Imagine that you are trying to explain the content of the video to a friend (ideally who represents or is similar to your customer avatar). Do it out loud while using the paper with the bullet points. Do it several times until you feel comfortable with the flow.

Step 4

Set up your phone, start recording, and present the full video from the beginning to the end. If you make a mistake, just keep going. If you forget about something, look down at the paper and keep talking. Do a maximum of three takes, and don't worry about making it perfect. After all, nobody will see it but you.

It's just for practice, so mess around and have fun with it. This is your chance to experiment with different styles and see what works best. For example, you could make one version of the video where you are quite serious and another one where you pretend that you are a bit intoxicated. The bottom line is this: The camera is your friend, and you are becoming better (and more comfortable) every time you practice.

Repeat the above steps for EVERY SINGLE video of the course until you have every lecture recorded.

WHAT HAPPENS NEXT?

You may be thinking that I will now tell you to watch each one of those pajama draft videos so you can critique yourself. Actually, I don't want you to even think about watching those. I know that this may sound confusing, so let me explain.

Since it's just a "dirty" draft for the sake of practice, those videos don't represent even a third of your potential. If you watch them to evaluate your performance, you risk baking in some self-doubts. You may look at yourself sitting in front of the camera in your sweat pants and think: "Eeee, I'm not ready to release my content to the world."

Instead, once you finish creating all the draft videos, I want you to simply celebrate that you've just put in more practice than 99.5% of all other aspiring content creators. You're already ahead of your competition in terms of the discipline you've exercised throughout your preparation. You have developed the mindset of a pro.

Now delete all those files and celebrate. You're ready for the real video shoot.

Congratulations! You've demonstrated to yourself that you have nothing to fear. The "unknown" suddenly has transformed into familiar territory. You know precisely what content you will share with your audience. You know how you will present it. There is absolutely nothing that can throw you out of balance, and this awareness is giving you a lot of confidence. Celebrate, take a few days off, and schedule the official video shoot knowing 100% that you CAN and WILL make it a success. You've already proven to yourself that you have what it takes.

Next up, we'll dive into publishing and marketing. Have no fear. Once again, we'll keep it simple.

THINGS TO REMEMBER

- Create a "pajama" draft of your course for practice, removing expectations and pressure. It allows you to fully focus on content and delivery.

- Film your draft in ridiculous clothing, subconsciously signaling to yourself that the videos won't be seen by anyone, thereby alleviating the pressure.

- Outline each lecture with bullet points, practice them out loud, and film a maximum of three takes. Rinse and repeat the process until your draft course is complete.

- Avoid watching your pajama draft videos to prevent any self-doubt from creeping in. Remember that it's just a practice round that doesn't represent your true potential.

- Delete your draft videos and celebrate! Recognize that you've put in more practice than most content creators. You've developed the mindset of a "pro."

- Schedule the official video shoot confidently, knowing you've already overcome fears and have become familiar with the content.

PART 5

PUBLISHING AND MARKETING FOR IMPACT AND PROFIT

I'll never forget the day I clicked the **Publish** button in Udemy for my first online course. It was New Year's Eve 2013, and I was celebrating in Budapest with friends. "Celebration" may not be entirely accurate, as I was in a lot of emotional pain. You see, just a few months earlier, a serious relationship had ended. Initially, I had felt fine, but the reality of the situation hit me belatedly like a steel hammer. Only a few days earlier, I had tried to get back together with my ex and was rejected. Whenever I was around people, I was trying to keep my shit together, but I could feel conflicting emotions swirling inside me. Adding to the emotional storm, my first online course, *Double Your Confidence and Self-Esteem*, was finally edited and ready to be published. I was about to find out if the market would accept me or if I was about to face more rejection.

I had quit my last job several months earlier. I had depleted my savings. I had a broken heart and no idea what the hell I was doing. The only thing I knew was that I had put my whole heart and soul into that course because I genuinely wanted to make a positive impact.

With some good friends standing behind me and sweat pouring down my forehead, I clicked "Publish." It was a surreal moment. On the one hand, I was excited. On the other, I was aware that what happened next would have a significant impact on my life, whether this worked or didn't work. *What if nobody buys it? What if people don't resonate with my content? Would that make me a total failure?*

That evening, my friends and I went to see the movie *The Wolf of Wall Street* to take some of the pressure off. On the way home, my stress levels began to increase rapidly. Back inside, my friends urged me to refresh my instructor dashboard. Everyone was curious about what we would see.

The growing pressure I felt put me in a state of near-paralysis. My lesser self kept whispering: *"What if not even one person enrolled in my course? What if this will never work?"* Finally, I pushed myself to face the truth. Do or die. I opened my laptop and studied the dashboard. According to my friends, an expression of shock, disbelief, and exhilaration overwhelmed my face. "No way! Some people already bought my course! I can't believe it!" I exclaimed.

I had been hoping for this outcome but in my wildest dreams didn't expect that sales would come in so quickly. I didn't quite know why, but I had a peculiar feeling that my life would never be the same.

Man, was I right!

Once I had a taste of what was possible I knew I wouldn't go back to the status quo. I felt like Neo after taking the red pill in *The Matrix*. Making my first online dollar by teaching what I'm passionate about was one of the most significant breakthroughs in my life.

Back then, I had no blueprint, no role models to show me the way. Sure, I had read many business and marketing books, but building online courses wasn't a "thing" back then. I didn't have anybody to guide me along the way. I was forced to learn how to fly *after* jumping off the cliff. The path wasn't easy. In fact, it took me six long months with a lot of hard work and sacrifices to break the $1,000 mark.

That's why I'm here to be your guide. I want to be the mentor I wish I had back then. In this chapter, I will share what I've learned about publishing and marketing your courses. Please bear in mind that the online course landscape is continually evolving, and there is no one right or wrong way to publish. Also, everyone has different objectives and circumstances. That said, I will do everything in my power to turn seemingly complex issues into simple action steps so you can make an educated decision on how to proceed.

CHAPTER 20

CHOOSING A PLATFORM

TYPES OF PLATFORMS

Whenever people ask me: **What is the best platform for publishing an online course?** My answer often surprises them. I explain that no platform is inherently the best. They simply ARE; which one is best for them depends on their personal situation and specific goals.

I've found that choosing between two types of vehicles serves as a good analogy. During my keynotes, I like to show people pictures of a new Bugatti and a new camper van. I then ask: "If I told you that I will give you one of those cars to use for five years, with the only stipulation being that you can't sell it, which one would you choose?"

You may be thinking that opting for a luxury sports car that costs at least $2 million would be an obvious choice, and yes, whenever

I speak to more traditional business audiences, the majority raise their hands when a picture of a brand new Bugatti flashes on the screen. However, the situation changes dramatically whenever I give presentations to digital nomads. Interestingly, most of them claim that they would rather pick a camper van. Why? Because many nomads don't care about how fancy the car is. They chose their full-time travel lifestyle for a reason; they love the idea of exploring the world in a brand new motorhome

Everything is relative, including your choice of online course platform. Many factors will determine which path makes the most sense for you. Here I'll break down different types of course platforms and the various factors you should consider to make an educated decision. My goal is not to bury you with lots of information as this is precisely what keeps aspiring creators confused. Instead, I will point out the key factors and considerations that will make it easier for you to make an intelligent (and quick) decision.

There are two main types of platforms to consider:

Volume-focused online marketplace platforms such as Udemy and Skillshare.

- PRO: Those platforms are easy to use, and excellent for getting exposure and free traffic thanks to their existing student base.

- CON: You have limited control. For instance, you can't collect email addresses directly.

Hosting platforms that give you full control and flexibility, but lack an existing marketplace, such as Thinkific, Kajabi, Teachable.

- PRO: You get complete flexibility in terms of your design, pricing, promotions, and direct access to email addresses of your customers.

- CON: These platforms don't offer a built-in marketplace. In essence, you get all the tools, but it's your job to find clients.

I'll explain each option in greater detail below. However, I strongly encourage you to sign up for free accounts to get a real "feel" for various platforms before making a decision. For an updated list of recommended platforms (by the time you read this book, there may be new promising players on the market), visit my resources page: **www.jimmynaraine.com/coursecreationresources**

VOLUME-FOCUSED ONLINE MARKETPLACE PLATFORMS

Volume platforms such as Udemy or Skillshare have a massive base of existing students. Why do I call them volume platforms? Well, it's because they have huge traffic, but the average price of the courses sold on them is relatively low. However, the great thing is that those platforms act as marketplaces that bring together content producers and buyers.

This option is especially attractive for someone who doesn't have a strong base of existing followers. For example, when I got started on Udemy, I didn't have an audience apart from a small number of YouTube subscribers. Thanks to finding an unfulfilled need in the market, my valuable content, and excellent video quality, my courses ended up being discovered daily by complete strangers—all due to the Udemy marketplace.

Looking back I can't imagine trying to get started by hosting my classes on a website built from scratch. In the first place, at that stage of my life, I had no idea how to create my own quality landing page, much less how to generate traffic online. I simply yearned to share my experience with those in need without getting confused by all the technical details. Attempting to do everything myself would've most probably resulted in little to no traction. It's been almost a decade since the moment I first went online and the world of online courses has progressed dramatically. Nowadays, it's so much easier to get started; there are plenty of resources and options at your disposal. However, if you don't have an existing audience, you may find the volume approach very compelling. As long as you follow this book's strategies and produce a high-quality course, people will discover it on those platforms. It's also an excellent way to start building your follower base and optimizing your content based on real-life feedback.

Each week, new up-and-coming marketplace platforms enter the course space to try to claim their share of the industry. However, to avoid confusion, let's stick to the major players that have solidified their position through the years as the best places to publish: Skillshare and Udemy.

Skillshare is a platform where students pay a fixed monthly subscription fee and get access to *all* the courses. How much money you make depends on the number of minutes students spend consuming your videos relative to all the other classes. Skillshare has an algorithm to calculate the instructor's revenue. I've never published anything on Skillshare for one simple reason. When Udemy started working exceptionally well for me, I didn't want to confuse my students with two completely different pricing models. Imagine someone buying several of my courses on Udemy, only to find that Skillshare grants access to all of them with a small monthly membership. Having said that, different things work for different people. If you are just getting started, I would recommend experimenting to see which platform works best for you. I know instructors who have been publishing with success on all available platforms from the start. There is really no inherent right or wrong here, it's a matter of your personal strategy.

Udemy is a course marketplace that has been growing like it's on steroids since its inception. When I released my first online course on December 31, 2013, Udemy had two million students. In 2023, this number had increased to more than 56 million. Even though I now own various products (from membership sites to joint courses with prominent brands), I'm still using Udemy as my main platform of choice. The reasons include its massive reach, smart promotions, friendly interface, intuitive instructor dashboard, and a sharp team that's on a mission to bring education to every home in the world. I even had the pleasure of visiting Udemy's office in San Francisco several years ago, so I've seen first-hand that the people there work very hard to take their company to the next level and to provide a positive experience for all involved. In 2022, Udemy officially recognized me as one of its Instructor Partners, and since then I've been in touch regularly with their team to figure out new ways to improve the instructor experience. Just like any platform Udemy has its flaws. However, after having many interactions with them, including the executive team, I can promise you that they genuinely care about their instructors and do their best to keep improving our teaching experience.

THINGS TO KEEP IN MIND ABOUT UDEMY

As I mentioned before, Udemy is a volume platform. This means their courses rarely sell at the listed price. Instead, Udemy runs a variety of promotions, including time-sensitive flash sales with prices as low as $9.99. Other promotions include student-specific offers such as purchasing an initial Udemy course at a steep discount. Bear in mind that as a creator you can opt-out of Udemy promotions, but I don't recommend it. No matter how good your content is, if you try to sell it at a premium price it will be virtually impossible to compete with thousands of other discounted products. As an instructor, you can also create various coupon codes for your audience. This includes free access passes that you can give to your friends and family (soon I will discuss how to take advantage of this).

Moreover, Udemy runs an affiliate program. If you create top-quality products it is more likely that you will appeal to potential affiliates. Udemy also focuses heavily on paid advertising. However, your courses have to be high quality and possess a solid track record to qualify for that part of the program.

Udemy keeps a percentage of your course sales, depending on the source. For example, as of February 2023, if Udemy successfully drives students to buy your course, it gets 63% of the revenue. Based on my experience of selling over half a million courses on Udemy, most customers pay between $10 and $25 for a course. When you do the math and subtract Udemy's percentage, you may wonder: "What's the point of publishing with Udemy, if sometimes I'll end up getting just a few bucks per sale!?" I feel your frustration, but there is something you need to consider. Whenever Udemy promotes your course, it's essentially free money to you. After all, they put in all the work managing the platform, running ads, and getting your course in front of potential customers. It makes sense for them to get a piece of the pie. You are passively collecting the payments.

This earnings-per-student issue makes some instructors angry. My response is always the same. Udemy is not forcing you to use their platform, so if you decide to do it, focus on what works. Sure, you may not be making a lot of money per student, but if you add up all of those enrollments, your monthly profit can become very healthy. It's not uncommon for instructors to make a full-time income from their courses. My Udemy courses have generated millions of dollars, and there are many other instructors who share my experience.

What's the split if you proactively promote your courses? Well, this is when the situation changes dramatically. If you refer a student to your online course, you retain pretty much the entire revenue (97%). Having said that, it's always wise to confirm the latest percentage splits before committing to any platform, as terms and conditions can change any time.

The main benefit for those of you starting from scratch is that on Udemy you automatically get exposure to potential clients. The site makes it simple for people with no pre-existing audience to gain traction. Naturally, like with anything in life, there are always trade-offs you need to consider.

FREEDOM

The great thing about Udemy, Skillshare, and many other platforms (including Thinkific, Teachable, and Kajabi, which we will discuss shortly) is that there is no exclusivity agreement that binds you. This means that you can publish your courses across the web as you wish.

For instance, I license some of my courses to companies for their internal use. In this case, we agree on a yearly, non-exclusive licensing fee, sign a contract, I submit my videos, and voila! They get access to my course, and I receive a nice fee without having to physically do anything.

If you want to start making deals like this, focus on building top-quality content and the customers will come. In terms of non-exclusivity, the one exception is **Udemy for Business**, which is a platform under Udemy's umbrella. If your class gets featured there, it cannot be sold on any competing platform (except your own website).

UDEMY FOR BUSINESS

Udemy for Business (UFB) is a subscription model for companies to give their employees on-demand access to top online courses. As with Skillshare, you get paid based on the number of minutes people spend watching your content. However, the UFB collection is optimized for developing professional skills. Udemy for Business has been growing rapidly and in early 2023 had almost 14,000 enterprise customers. Many of my courses are listed in the UFB program.

Not all courses are eligible to be on UFB. The reason is that Udemy is trying to maintain an exceptionally high standard for its corporate clients. Therefore, only products with the minimum number of high ratings are considered. Unfortunately, the process of joining Udemy for Business is not straightforward as there is no official application process. However, the UFB curation team constantly scans the regular Udemy marketplace looking for well-established, high-rated courses to feature in the business collection.

If you want to maximize the probability that your classes will get selected, create top-quality content that specifically targets corporate audiences and… patiently wait for Udemy's "congratulations" email. The more high-quality, business-related courses you publish on Udemy the higher the probability that you will get on the curation team's radar. I'm aware that it all sounds vague, but this is how the system works. Even Udemy Instructor Partners are not automatically admitted to the Udemy for Business collection. However, it is worth patiently trying to "join the club" since UFB will also open other opportunities. For instance, I've done multiple corporate presentations for huge companies thanks to being discovered in the Udemy for Business collection.

PLATFORMS THAT GIVE YOU MORE CONTROL, BUT NO MARKETPLACE

As I said earlier, if you are just starting your journey with course creation and have no existing audience, Udemy and Skillshare can be great choices. However, if you don't resonate with their offering, the three most prominent alternatives are **Thinkific, Kajabi, and Teachable**. The main difference with these platforms is they are not designed as a marketplace. This may change (I hope so) in the future, of course, but currently, they serve more as a solution for *designing and hosting* your online courses. They provide some marketing tools, but it's completely up to you if and how you utilize them. It means that you will not make any money by simply uploading your videos to these platforms. Instead, you'll need to personally engage in marketing efforts to send quality traffic to your landing page.

Kajabi, Thinkific, and Teachable don't work to draw an audience to your courses the way Udemy or Skillshare do. However, they are excellent for creating your own online school ecosystem.

While all marketing efforts will be up to you, there are some tremendous benefits to using these types of hosting platforms. First of all, you can customize your course page in whatever way you desire and charge whatever price you feel is fair (with all types of custom discounts). You can also create course bundles, a membership site where people pay you monthly for access to your content, online coaching packages, and more. You also get full access to email addresses provided by your students. Thanks to this, you can contact them anytime to promote whatever you please. This feature is something that Udemy and Skillshare don't offer. On Udemy, you can contact your students only by sending emails directly via your instructor dashboard, and promoting outside products is not allowed (apart from mentioning them ONLY in the final lecture of your course). On Skillshare, you can only create announcements within the platform.

Finally, it's important to note that Kajabi is slightly different from other platforms. At first glance, their membership packages may seem expensive. However, you need to be aware that you get what you pay for, and Kajabi is a holistic online course solution where you can build your entire business under one roof. Unlike other course platforms, Kajabi is a hybrid of a website builder (including membership sites), hosting platform, an email marketing system, and more. Once you invest in Kajabi there is really no need to purchase any additional software. There are plenty of creators out there who run their entire online businesses solely on Kajabi.

WHEN SHOULD YOU CONSIDER USING THINKIFIC, KAJABI OR TEACHABLE?

Platforms such as Thinkific, Kajabi, or Teachable can be an excellent option for creators who have an existing audience ready to buy. They are also optimal for those who are willing to handle their own marketing with a lot of flexibility. This is especially true when you want to fully customize your offering, from building unique landing pages and setting premium prices, to running all types of fully customized promotional campaigns.

For example, suppose you build a comprehensive masterclass that you plan to sell to your already established audience for $197 with the original (reference) price set at $497. This wouldn't be possible on a marketplace platform like Udemy or Skillshare as they would devalue your content by running their own promotions. Therefore, in this scenario, it's a no-brainer to use a solution such as Thinkific, Kajabi, or Teachable. However, be aware that if you don't have an existing audience or a precise way of getting warm leads to that landing page, things can get tricky. After all, you may have an extremely valuable course worth top dollar, but how can you expect anyone to enroll if nobody knows it even exists?

IMPORTANT CONSIDERATION IF YOU DON'T HAVE AN EXISTING AUDIENCE

If you don't have an existing audience, but are considering using Teachable, Thinkific, or Kajabi, start building your following ASAP. I know individuals who didn't have an existing fan base but started forming the foundation during their course creation process. They released various content pieces long before their course launch, from posting social media videos and running live training, to writing value-packed articles. They then used smart marketing funnels (more about that soon) to propel their viewers to subscribe for some kind of free content. This strategy enabled them to collect email addresses from appreciative audience. Later, during the course launch, they managed to capitalize on the pre-built list of people they had already provided value to.

This approach can certainly work, but it requires a *lot* of discipline and consistency. Let's face reality. Occasional social media posts will not hack it. Building an audience from scratch requires effort and consistency (more now than ever). The times of getting thousands of likes on your organic posts are long gone, as social media platforms are overcrowded and have been aggressively moving towards a "pay for play" approach. It is still possible to grow your social media (and email list) organically, but if you think it's just a walk in the park you are in for a rude awakening. It will take a substantial amount of time and consistent effort, but if you stick with it, you will see results. If you don't have any following yet, certainly don't dwell on the fact that you "should've started earlier." Instead, begin the process right away. There are certain strategies you can use to "hack" your progress, for instance, leveraging people with existing audiences through win-win partnerships. More about that later.

Naturally, you could also speed up your progress dramatically by working with an experienced online marketer, carving out some advertising budget. Of course, most people are not willing (or cannot afford) to do that from the start. This is why, if just thinking about all of this overwhelms you, I recommend that you initially stick to marketplace platforms in order to release your course as soon as possible and get your feet "wet." The experience will teach you more than reading any book, and in the process, you will be able to calibrate what you really want.

THE BEST OF BOTH WORLDS

Alternatively, you could use Thinkific, Kajabi, or Teachable combined with a marketplace platform such as Udemy in a **hybrid model**. To do this, you could publish a regular version of your course(s) on Udemy, and then publish a bigger (and more expensive) masterclass on a platform such as Thinkific. This way, you get the best of both worlds.

For instance, you could start by creating a 45 to 60 minute free Udemy course to get the initial traction in terms of student sign-ups and reviews (and to get valuable feedback). You could then start gradually releasing those same videos on social media, letting your audience know that if they sign up for your email newsletter, you will give them free access to that course. While this audience could just find your free Udemy course without signing up on your email list, most of them will not proactively look into it. If the course resonates with them, they will most likely give you their email addresses in exchange for having quick access to all your videos in one place. This is especially true if you offer some type of extra bonus for signing up to your email list, such as PDF or a checklist.

This way you get two wins. First, you drive your regular social media traffic to your email list, which you can then monetize however you please. Second, you are semi-passively building your new following on Udemy, learning a lot in the process, and gaining credibility on the platform. Then, once you feel ready, you can release a more comprehensive (and higher-priced) course on Thinkific, Kajabi, or Teachable and start offering it to your email subscribers, on social media channels, and in your last lecture of your free Udemy course.

With this strategy, you ensure that all your followers across the web have something to choose from. Most of them won't be interested in financially committing to your premium masterclass, but may be excited to sign up on your email list in exchange for a free course with bonuses. As they get more familiar with your content and brand, some of them may eventually buy your premium course. In the meantime, you'll be taking advantage of all the free traffic the Udemy/Skillshare marketplaces provide. Overall, a hybrid strategy like this is an easy way to "taste" both worlds without getting paralyzed by confusion.

EXCLUSIVE PLATFORM ALTERNATIVES

Just to make sure you are aware of all the options out there, I'll briefly touch on course platforms that most creators won't use, but should know about.

First, depending on your profile, you could aim to land a partnership with one of the "elite" course platforms such as Coursera, Masterclass, or Mindvalley. However, bear in mind that the gateways to entry on these sites are well-guarded. For instance, Masterclass creates high-quality in-house courses only with very well known public figures. Some of their instructors include Dan Brown, Neil deGrasse Tyson, Carlos Santana, Marc Jacobs, and even a couple of former U.S. Presidents. In order to teach on Coursera you need to be an established professor at one of the world's leading universities. Finally, Mindvalley chooses their instructors based on a variety of factors including brand alignment, the size of their following, and how their expertise fills the gaps in Mindvalley's (already comprehensive) offerings.

Does all of this mean that you shouldn't aim to teach on those platforms? Of course not! I'm a true believer in thinking BIG. However, remember that the best way to get on those platforms' radar is to build a powerful brand and a track record of helping huge numbers of people. Hence, your best bet is to get started with the "mainstream" platforms and consistently do your best to succeed.

Second, in order to get total control and flexibility you could build your own site from scratch, completely disregarding existing course platforms, using only selected plugins and custom code. However, this approach requires a *lot* more effort, tech skills, financial investment, and nerves of steel. If you embark on this path, you are very much on your own, for example, being responsible for fixing any technical issues that may arise. Only a tiny percentage of (usually very experienced and already successful) people would genuinely entertain this option considering the immense value that the existing platforms provide relative to their monthly cost. Hence, exploring this option is beyond the scope of this book. Besides, I doubt that if you're considering going the independent route you would be reading a book with the word "SIMPLIFIED" in the title.

THINGS TO REMEMBER

- Your platform choice depends on your specific needs. There is no right or wrong.

- Evaluate platform trade-offs. Are you after instant exposure vs. more control?

- Examples of volume-focused online marketplaces with limited control are Udemy and Skillshare.

- Examples of hosting platforms that provide complete control but lack a marketplace are Thinkific, Kajabi, and Teachable.

- Register your free account on various platforms to see which one you resonate with the most.

- Most online course platforms are non-exclusive, allowing you to publish the same content elsewhere.

- If you are willing to do your own marketing, and your priority is control and complete customization, consider Thinkific, Kajabi, or Teachable.

- If you want to publish online courses fast, and tap into an existing marketplace, consider Udemy and Skillshare.

- Building a big audience requires discipline, consistency, and strategic partnerships.

- Consider a hybrid model combining various platforms to maximize your flexibility and exposure.

- If you have limited time and tend to procrastinate, start with a short course on Udemy to "get your feet wet." Remember that you can always create more courses on other platforms, but at least you will have started.

- Start building your email list today by offering different content pieces for free to those who sign up.

- Cultivate a flexible and adaptable mindset as the online course industry continuously evolves.

CHAPTER 21

UNDERSTANDING THE BASICS OF SALES FUNNELS

Let's briefly talk about **marketing funnels** to help you determine *how* to position your course in your online ecosystem. Neil Patel, one of the smartest marketers out there, defines a funnel as "the set of steps a visitor needs to go through before they can reach the conversion." In other words, it's your customer's journey with you from point of contact to point of sale (and beyond).

In some ways, a marketing funnel is similar to dating. When you meet someone for the first time you don't nonchalantly ask: "Hey, let's go camping for a week, just the two of us!" Instead, you may start with a relaxed coffee date or some fun activity like roller-blading. If you click, you may meet for dinner several days later. Eventually, after a series of dates and getting to know each other, you may decide to take a bigger step and spend a night together.

That's kind of how the customer journey works. You may be offering a ton of value, but when people see your content for the first time, they'll be unlikely to sign up for your expensive masterclass or a coaching package. You haven't established enough trust, credibility, and familiarity for them to take the leap yet. You need to design a customer journey in such a way that doesn't make them feel like they are going camping with you on your first date.

Now that you have a basic understanding of the purpose of a funnel, let's discuss it in the context of creating an online business. Instead of trying to sell a premium product or service the moment someone discovers your content, first offer them something that is easy for them to accept. It could be a value-packed gift, such as a free eBook, a PDF "cheat sheet," or complimentary access to a mini video course. Since you are providing pure value without expecting anything in return, people are more likely to give it a shot.

After becoming more familiar with your content, some of those individuals may then feel compelled to enroll in your $10 to $25 course. That's the point at which most people will stop. However, those who truly resonate with your content may feel ready to sign up for your more expensive masterclass.

Gradually, the relationship gets stronger. As long as you keep exceeding expectations, some of your clients will keep going deeper into your funnel. Eventually, they may be interested in your premium offering, from coaching to attending your live events. If you want to learn more about this subject, I recommend *Dotcom Secrets*, by Russel Brunson. In my opinion he is the top expert on building funnels.

A fundamental understanding of how funnels work will help you to decide how your content should be positioned in the mind of your customer. If you are just getting started, please don't let any of this overcomplicate things for you. In fact, when I got started, I didn't know a thing about funnels. I simply published my classes on Udemy and focused on creating as much value as possible for my students. There will always be more to learn, but ultimately, the most important thing is that you get your course out there ASAP.

THINGS TO REMEMBER

- A marketing funnel is a customer journey from the moment they find out about you to the point of sale and beyond.

- Continuously strive to keep increasing trust and credibility.

- Start with free, value-packed offerings (eBooks, PDFs, mini-courses) to easily attract and engage new audiences at scale.

- Ultimately aim to offer various products catering to different customer commitment levels, from affordable courses to premium offerings.

- Don't overthink things. Launch your first course ASAP, and refine your funnel strategy as you grow.

- Guide customers through different commitment levels, from affordable courses to premium masterclasses and coaching.

CHAPTER 22

BUSINESS STRATEGY BASED ON YOUR PRIMARY OBJECTIVE

In this chapter, I will take you through examples of business and marketing strategies you could embrace, particularly what to focus on based on your primary objective. I'm doing this to give you some ideas, but please bear in mind that there is no inherent right or wrong, like in math or physics. The strategy you choose will depend on your circumstances and preferences. Also, it's worth repeating that choosing one strategy over others is not like getting a neck tattoo. You are not setting anything in stone; the beautiful thing about the online space is that everything can be amended and further optimized. Therefore, please do your best to avoid the chains of the paradox of choice.

PRIMARY OBJECTIVE: CREATING A STREAM OF PASSIVE INCOME

If your biggest priority is financial success, there are a few things you need to consider. First of all, always exceed expectations in terms of the value you provide. In other words, if you are charging $100 for your course, make sure that your customer gets at least $1,000 worth of value. Under this objective, let's discuss two options for selling your courses.

Option 1: Full focus on Udemy

One path is to embrace **the high-volume/low-price approach** by regularly creating medium-length (60 to 180 minutes) **Udemy** courses. This way, whenever you release a new product, you can immediately promote it to your growing Udemy audience. This is precisely how I started, and it's worked out well for me.

Keep in mind that while you can assign any listing price to your course, Udemy is a **volume platform** that relies on promotions. The actual amount that your customers pay per course may be anywhere from $10 and $25. That fee is determined by Udemy's promotion strategy—not by you. This approach is excellent for any beginner because Udemy exposes your classes to their database of 56 million students, handles the paid advertising, and takes care of collecting payments (and paying you).

Bear in mind that the extent to which they promote your content depends on demand for your topic, the quality of your course and conversion rates. Naturally, courses with outstanding content, lots of five-star reviews, and well-optimized landing pages (with strong keywords) will appear higher in search rankings. Also, remember, with this kind of model, the more courses you create, the higher your chance of generating revenue. In fact, I encourage you to treat Udemy a little bit like YouTube. Instead of spending six months or more creating an extensive, comprehensive course (that may or may not work well), it makes more sense to divide your knowledge into one- to three-hour courses and post them regularly. This approach allows you to create multiple courses each year, see which ones work best, and then double down on those. In my career, I had situations where I started with 60-minute and even 40-minute courses, waited for the feedback and further optimized based on that feedback. I would then see which course(s) performed best and kept supplying more content to those. Instead of blindly assuming that something would definitely work, I kept testing and choosing my shots carefully. This is the embodiment of the Pareto Principle, which asserts that roughly 80% of your results come from 20% of causes. In other words, very few things really matter. The best way to create leverage in your course business (and life in general) is to identify the "vital few" and double down on those game-changing actions.

Option 2: Premium masterclass

Your second option under this objective is to create **a longer, premium masterclass** hosted on a platform that gives you full control of your pricing model, such as **Thinkific, Kajabi, or Teachable**. You can sell your course at a much higher price, whether it's $200, $500, or more. Your sales results will naturally depend on various factors such as your ability to drive well-targeted traffic, as well as your brand credibility, social proof, landing page quality, money-back guarantee policy, etc.

If done correctly, this option gives you a lot of potential to generate income. However, it's more complex and requires significantly more effort than simply uploading your videos to an existing marketplace such as Udemy. If you don't resonate with the volume platform model, don't want a platform to heavily discount your courses, and want to primarily concentrate on building your own ecosystem, this option is for you. However, if this is what you want to go for, I highly encourage you to follow the advice I provided earlier. Get started ASAP with building up your social media following and especially growing your email marketing ecosystem.

PRIMARY OBJECTIVE: GAINING CREDIBILITY IN YOUR INDUSTRY

If **credibility** is what you're after, remember that if you host a course outside of the major marketplace platforms (such as Udemy), nobody will see your official stats and ratings. Sure, you can add testimonials to your landing page, but since you fully control what shows up there, everyone knows that you can freely alter the actual numbers. When you have a course on Udemy, everyone knows your numbers are real. For that reason, platforms such as Udemy serve as credibility boosters. It's in your best interest to maximize your number of students and even more importantly, the ratings. Let's look at how you can achieve this.

QUICKEST WAY TO BOOST SOCIAL PROOF

If you're like most people, you probably have limited time and resources to invest in building your course. At the same time, you want to maximize your perceived value, credibility, and potential reach. You can move toward these goals by creating **a flagship course** on a platform such as Udemy. Then, for a limited time during your launch, you can release a free access code for your family, friends, or select communities. Make sure to emphasize the scarcity of this gesture, making clear that it's a **limited-time offer**. By doing this you're likely to enroll hundreds, perhaps even more than a thousand people, in your course right away and obtain several early five-star reviews.

The goal of this strategy is to create instant credibility. You will not make any money on viewers using free access codes, and a lot of those people may not actively participate in your lectures. But this strategy will help you because anybody visiting your landing page will be influenced by the **social proof** you've just engineered. They'll take note of the number of people who have enrolled in your course. These new potential students will be more likely to feel comfortable paying for your course for one simple reason—nobody wants to be the first buyer, the guinea pig. Moreover, creating this initial social proof will make you more likely to book speaking gigs and podcast interviews, which will then drive extra traffic to your course/s. This is how you engineer a positive upward spiral early on.

Here's another powerful strategy for building social proof. When you deal with potential clients, business partners, or conference organizers, send them a link to your landing page. Tell them that you would love to give them free access if a course topic resonates with them. If they turn down your offer at least they've seen your landing page, which displays important credibility factors. If their answer is: "Yes," make sure you generate a unique coupon code with their name in it. This way, they'll know that the access code was created just for them, which increases the perceived value. You may be wondering: "So what's the point in giving them complimentary access?" First, if they watch your videos, your brand will be further solidified in their minds. Second, they will be more likely to do something for you in the future due to the **reciprocity effect**.

PRIMARY OBJECTIVE: MAXIMUM IMPACT

If you prioritize your **global reach** over anything else, there's a different approach on the menu. You could create a series of value-packed courses and release them all over the internet, for free. Most course platforms don't retain exclusivity rights to your content, meaning you can repurpose it anywhere you want. Even though this approach will not produce any direct income, it will allow you to maximize your worldwide impact and gain credibility very quickly.

Imagine having 10,000 people taking your free courses versus teaching 100 paid students. Naturally, in the second scenario, you are generating income. However, if money is not your primary goal, this may be a better option as it offers you much more impact. Besides, imagine the expression on peoples' faces when they see that you teach 10,000 people! Sometimes it's better to use your courses as leverage versus as a direct income stream.

PARALYZED BY THE PARADOX OF CHOICE? HERE'S MY ADVICE.

Over the years, I've consulted with thousands of aspiring course creators at different events across the world. Whenever I ask them about their biggest stumbling blocks, many admit that they experience the paradox of choice. It is overwhelming to have so many options. Instead of focusing on creating a fantastic course, many individuals get stuck in research mode, resulting in perpetual indecision. "I'm still not sure if I should go with platforms A, B, or C. I suppose I just need to read more about it."

Sound familiar? I'm a big believer in getting people from 0 to 1 without overcomplicating matters. So, here's what I recommend if you lack clarity.

Unless you have a pre-existing audience and a solid strategy, publish your first course on Udemy. Aim for one hour of videos, and just get it done! Don't wrestle too much with choosing the "ideal" strategy. That will only lead to **paralysis by analysis**, and you may never pull the trigger. Instead, focus on producing the best content you are capable of creating and get your course out there! You can then experiment by repurposing your first course on different platforms to see what works for YOU. You can always adjust later. All the other options will still be available to you. What matters the most is that you get started. Your target audience needs you.

Apart from creating a quality course, address students' feedback early on. If several people give you the same suggestion for improving the user experience, implement it right away. If your customers are asking for additional videos, film them. If several people clearly say that PDF summaries would make the course better, provide those. The point is that you have to imagine yourself in the shoes of your customers and make sure that they love your product. This approach will translate into better ratings, which in turn will attract even more students.

THINGS TO REMEMBER

- Choose a business strategy based on your primary objective: passive income, credibility, or maximum impact.

- Passive Income - Option 1: Focus on creating medium-length courses on Udemy, leveraging their promotional efforts and large user base.

- Passive Income - Option 2: Develop a premium masterclass on platforms like Thinkific, Kajabi, or Teachable, retaining complete control over pricing and marketing.

- To gain social proof and credibility as quickly as possible, publish on Udemy and offer free access codes to boost initial student numbers and reviews.

- Offer free course access to potential clients/partners to stand out, leverage the reciprocity effect, and build credibility.

- For maximum impact, create free/low-cost courses and distribute them everywhere.

- Don't let the paradox of choice paralyze you. If in doubt, start by publishing your first course on Udemy and adjust your strategy along the way.

- Take student feedback seriously, and address it promptly to enhance user experience and boost ratings.

CHAPTER 23

PRE-LAUNCH STRATEGIES

Contrary to popular belief, publishing your course doesn't start when you go live. If you want to maximize your opportunities, you need to start working on your launch long before you click that magic "publish" button. In this chapter we'll discuss some essential elements of your pre-launch strategy.

CLEAR PLAN AND MAXIMUM EFFORT

The biggest mistake you need to avoid is simply "dumping" your videos on one of the platforms, publishing your course, and waiting passively for the buyers to come. Instead, you should spend time before the launch to build a solid foundation to trigger a snowball effect. Unless you are Apple releasing the latest iPhone, nobody wants to be the first person to buy a brand new product, right? Imagine if someone stumbles upon your beautiful landing page, but your course has zero enrollments and zero reviews.

Even though the content may look valuable to them, they are not very likely to register.

It's the same psychological principle that makes people choose a nearly full restaurant over an empty one. As humans, we are continually looking for social proof to make our buying decisions. This is why you should engineer as much social proof as possible *before* you ever publish your class. To achieve this, you'll need to take several steps to build your audience, acquire early feedback, and optimize your promotional materials.

CULTIVATE YOUR INNER CIRCLE

Instead of relying on strangers to get started, begin with your circle of friends (and perhaps, trusted partners and colleagues). Start messaging people who match your target audience and tell them you're about to release a course. What I recommend is that you don't try to sell them anything. Ultimately, it's up to you how you choose to approach this situation. However, I believe that the potential benefit of selling is much smaller than the potential damage to the relationship. If you've ever been contacted out of the blue by an old friend trying to convince you to get that "incredible deal," you know what I mean. Instead, I encourage you to provide a lot of value to selected friends by offering them free access to your new class. It's crucial to be clear that you are making an exception for friendship's sake, and that you'd appreciate their honest feedback (and a formal course review).

Following is an example of a message you could send:

> *Hi <insert first name>,*
>
> *It's been a long time, and I hope that life is great on your side! I just wanted to let you know that I'm very excited,*

but also a bit nervous, because for the first time in my life, I'm releasing an online course about <subject>. I've put a lot of effort into making it as valuable as possible.

We've known each other for a long time, and I'm aware that you are interested in this topic. As your friend, I would love to gift you free access. I know that you will find some golden nuggets in there.

Let me know if it sounds exciting;)

If you get a positive response, let them know when the course will be published and promise that you will follow up with a free coupon code. To manage this process make sure to create a spreadsheet and track all the people you reach out to.

Once you publish your class, send them the promised access code, and remind them that it would be fantastic if they could leave a formal review. Emphasize the fact that even a one-word review will help you a lot, and it won't take more than 20 seconds.

Ideally, send them a personalized and upbeat audio/video message or call them to make it even more personal. This way, your inner circle will be more likely to support you. Besides, by speaking to each individual directly, you will also avoid any potential misunderstanding.

Naturally, there is no right or wrong approach. You should customize your message according to your circumstances. For example, you could be extremely direct with your closest friends, letting them know that this is the one time when you really need to rely on their support. You could ask them to not only take your course and leave a review on the day of the launch but also to share the landing page on their social media channels.

The extent to which you can comfortably use this strategy depends on how strong your friendships are. Personally, I no longer ask anyone for favors like this as I now have an established audience. However, a little support was always appreciated when I was getting started and went a long way to create the initial social proof. I encourage you to try that as well.

Getting your network to aid your launch will help you to build credibility right away because your landing page will no longer show zero students and reviews. Instead, you will have some five-star ratings right from the beginning. This, in itself, will make your course so much more attractive in the eyes of those who don't know you. Remember, gaining social proof is a game changer.

START BUILDING YOUR SOCIAL MEDIA FOLLOWING

If you don't have a social media presence, it's never too late to start. While the best time to get started was yesterday, the second-best time is now. Clearly, you have decided to embark on a journey to produce your first course; otherwise, you wouldn't be this far in the book. As you are building your course, take time to set up various social media accounts and begin sharing pieces of content related to your course topic. If you're not sure what type of material to share, use your curriculum to come up with quotes, teaching points, or interesting graphics. I also encourage you to create a frequently asked questions (FAQ) list that will make the content generation process more manageable.

Before we speak about specific things you can do, I need to address the "elephant in the room." I know what you may be thinking: "Come on, Jimmy. I plan to publish a course in a few weeks. What's the point of building an audience now? It's already too late."

Truth be told, with this type of thinking, you will never build an audience. In reality, even one week is better than nothing. Some of your biggest fans will end up being those who follow you from the very beginning. And yes, I'm speaking from experience. People enjoy the feeling of being a part of someone's journey. They love witnessing your transformation firsthand. It's this feeling that often turns them into loyal fans. To this day when I attend conferences around the world, I meet people who have been watching my lectures for five, six, even nine years. Remember that every single person you touch counts so begin building your audience today!

Finally, I know that it may feel discouraging when you get only ten subscribers in your first week, but guess what? Not a long time ago, those people didn't even know you existed! Rather than thinking about the number, visualize talking to these ten real human beings at your dinner table. This will help put things in perspective. You will also notice that as you become more successful, it's often easy to forget that the numbers represent real humans. Have you ever noticed that those with a fear of heights usually have no problem looking out of a plane's window? The reason is when you're so high above the ground your mind sees everything almost like a painting; you find it difficult to process the reality of the 30,000 feet between you and the ground. By the same token, as you start growing your following, your numbers may start to feel hard to process, almost unreal. In those moments, remind yourself that each number and each name represents a real human being.

THINGS TO REMEMBER

- Avoid the common mistake of assuming that buyers will come once you launch your course. Instead of passively hoping, do your best in the pre-launch phase and maintain your momentum post-launch.

- Cultivate your inner circle by offering free access to friends and diplomatically asking for honest feedback and course reviews.

- Send personalized, authentic messages to individuals from your inner circle to ensure their support.

- Start building hype around your course launch on social media in the pre-launch phase.

- Remember that every new follower/student counts. Visualize them as real people to maintain perspective and motivation.

CHAPTER 24

SEVEN SOCIAL MEDIA AND ORGANIC MARKETING STRATEGIES

In this chapter, I will share with you seven powerful social media and organic marketing strategies that will help you launch your product with a "bang" and keep growing your online business. Don't feel the need to pursue all of these ideas right away. I'm simply laying out some effective options for you. Unless you have a team, it's difficult to play full out on all fronts. However, it is true that the more you do, the better results you can expect. Start with the strategy that resonates with you the most, and over time you can add more to your repertoire. Remember that you don't need to be on all social media channels 24/7, as long as what you do, you do with a clear intent. For example, I enjoy posting content on Instagram, but I don't even have an active Twitter account. For some reason, I don't resonate with short text updates, and that's okay.

When deciding which channel or channels to tackle first, consider where your target audience is hanging out. If you are teaching a serious business topic, LinkedIn could be your best bet. If you're teaching photography, Instagram may be your place. On the other hand, if you are a dance teacher or stand-up comedian, you may do extremely well on a platform such as TikTok or YouTube.

Also, remember the importance of consistency. If you want to make things happen, you have to keep posting engaging content no matter what. It's enough if you post something once a week (although 3x would be optimal), but at least be consistent instead of sharing several content pieces within the period of a week and then forgetting about the platform for two months. Consistency is the key. I've learned this lesson the hard way. Nowadays, I have a team of people who edit my content and post it on social media on my behalf. I still take the time to interact with my audience, and do occasional live videos, but I no longer need to worry about the backend aspects of running social media accounts. This leaves me more room to focus on what's truly important—deep work, continuously improving my content, and optimizing my other business ventures.

Here are seven simple, yet powerful social media and organic marketing strategies you should consider embracing as you embark on your course creation journey:

- Immediately start building your email list.
- Regularly publish videos across social media platforms.
- Develop authentic relationships with podcasters.
- Contact bloggers and affiliates who review online courses.
- Talk to other creators in your niche.
- Become active in relevant online groups.
- Say YES! to all speaking engagements and record them.

Let's discuss how each one of these strategies can dramatically help you with your exposure and promotional efforts.

IMMEDIATELY START BUILDING YOUR EMAIL LIST

One of the biggest mistakes I made was not building my email list early enough. It's something that often feels overly complicated, especially with new General Data Protection Regulation (GDPR) laws. Fortunately, you can learn powerful email marketing software (e.g. Active Campaign, ConvertKit, MailChimp, and even Kajabi's native email system) relatively quickly. All of these services offer free tutorials. If in doubt, you can find plenty of instructional videos on YouTube or… take an affordable online course on Udemy.

Use your email list to communicate with the people who resonate with your content. I made the mistake of thinking that having subscribers on social media was enough. However, oftentimes, this is an illusion because many of your followers also follow hundreds or thousands of other content creators. If for whatever reason you want to contact them directly, it becomes virtually impossible without having their email addresses because you are at the mercy of the social media platforms to alert them to your message. After all, their algorithms are set up in such a way that most of your followers will usually not see your fresh content.

Having said that, it's harder than ever to convince people to willingly provide their email addresses. In our world of constant overstimulation, spam messages, and get rich quick scams, people want to protect their privacy (and sanity). To get their email addresses, you first need to gain trust and provide some serious value.

In the past, it was often enough to entice people with access to your free newsletter. Nowadays, if you want to stand out from the competition, you need to come across as trustworthy and provide what marketers call a **lead magnet**. This is some content that offers so much value that your potential customer finds it irresistible. In essence, it's like a strong magnet that pulls people in.

You can use various types of lead magnets to build your list. For example, you could give free access to a book you've written, a high-value checklist, or even a short online course. The person's potential benefit needs to exceed the cost of giving up some privacy. There are many books about email marketing. Delving into the nitty-gritty is beyond the scope of this book. As long as you remember this key rule, you'll do better than most of your competitors: GIVE more than you GET.

Remember that people who sign up for your email list are those who value your content and feel a high degree of trust. Once you launch your course, you can contact them immediately, offering either free access or a big discount (depending on your strategy).

REGULARLY PUBLISH VIDEOS ACROSS SOCIAL MEDIA PLATFORMS

Even though it's not easy to get started on social media, it is essential in today's market. As the world continues its shift more and more into the digital space, social media is where everyone is hanging out. It's a great place to start engaging with people who consume your content.

The good news is that publishing across several platforms doesn't have to be very time-consuming because you can repurpose content across channels. For example, whenever I post a video on YouTube, I also publish it on IGTV and Facebook. Since it's the same video, I simply copy and paste the title and description. To make matters even easier, you can use free software such as Buffer to assist you with pre-scheduling your content across various social media. And, if you have spare cash, you could outsource some of your social media work to a freelancer. If you resonate with this option, I recommend Upwork for finding and managing talent. As I mentioned earlier in the book, Upwork has plenty of freelancers to choose from, services are suitable for all budgets, and the platform is very easy to navigate. In fact, I've found some of my best employees there.

DEVELOP AUTHENTIC RELATIONSHIPS WITH PODCASTERS

Trying to land a guest spot on podcasts is something you should definitely consider, as it will give you evergreen exposure to a brand new audience. Many people don't have the time to browse online videos, because they are swamped with their day-to-day tasks. However, folks do spend a lot of time driving in their cars, cooking, working out, and pursuing other activities that don't require their full mental attention. As a result, listening to podcasts is their education of choice. If you get on podcasts you will expose yourself to people who otherwise wouldn't even find out that you exist. Although many of them may have never considered taking a course, they may get inspired to do so after listening to your episode.

Towards the end of most podcasts, the host usually asks: "So... where can people find you?" This is your golden opportunity to tell the audience about your course business. In fact, experienced podcast hosts try to do their best to "plug" your offering much earlier in the conversation too. This is pure gold as it appears more natural in conversation and increases the likelihood that the listeners will visit your course landing page(s).

I encourage you to find podcasters in your niche and reach out to them. Here are some tips for landing podcast interviews:

Do your research before sending out a pitch.

- Be concise yet compelling when reaching out to hosts. Read your email out loud before sending it to make sure it "sounds" right.

- In order to stand out, you can send them a custom video or audio message. If you pursue this option, make it as short and captivating as possible.

- Make their lives easier by mentioning specific topics you could discuss and how your talking points relate to their key audience.

- Don't focus on what you want to promote. Instead, concentrate on what's in it for them and their audience. Show them how you can bring value to their show.

- Once you lock in the interview, focus purely on giving your all. Impressing their audience with valuable content is the best form of marketing.

- Podcast hosts are busy. Don't get discouraged if you don't receive any response right away. Wait a week or two, and then message them again with a courteous follow-up.

- Provide value to the host right away. It could be as simple as leaving a five-star review on their podcast, product or service, tagging them in social media posts, or introducing them to a key collaborator. Content creators appreciate reviews tremendously, so believe me when I say that this WILL make you stand out.

- Don't limit yourself to targeting only the major players. Start with smaller podcasters and build yourself up gradually. There are plenty of fun, up-and-coming podcasts you could jump on to gain experience.

- Finally, once you land that podcast gig, remember about something crucial. The moment your episode is released you should promote it as much as possible driving lots of web traffic to the host. This shows other potential podcasters that you do your part till the end. Besides, it's the best way to thank the podcast host for inviting you.

CONTACT BLOGGERS AND AFFILIATES WHO REVIEW ONLINE COURSES

Search for sites and blogs that review products in your niche. Contact them, letting them know about your course. As always, focus on what's in it for them. For example, you could offer a limited number of free coupons for the members of their audience. Remember, whenever you provide value first, you have a higher chance of winning (a philosophy that applies to all realms of life).

TALK TO OTHER CREATORS IN YOUR NICHE

You may be thinking: "Is he asking me to make friends with my competition?!" The short answer is, Yes. I believe in collaboration. Instead of living in scarcity, acting as if everyone is trying to take away your bread, you can choose to live in abundance. Why not be friendly with people in your niche? This new mindset may even allow you to create fruitful collaborations.

For example, I helped my father and some friends build products that could be perceived as my direct competition. I don't see it this way, though. I feel like every instructor has a distinct style that will attract a different type of audience. One smart strategy that I would like to offer you is contacting people who create content that slightly overlaps with yours. This way, you have potentially useful interests in common, but you don't have direct competition for the same audience.

I once partnered with the Canadian memory champion, Anthony Metivier. We ended up building a course on habit creation. Another example is the *Physical & Mental Self-Defense* course I developed with my very good friend, Ilya Grad (yes, the same Ilya who is a three-time world champion in Thai boxing). Even though it may seem like we operate in two different worlds, there's an interesting overlap. I teach how to build confidence, courage, and cultivate mental strength. Ilya teaches people how to fight and defend themselves. We combined our knowledge and experiences into a bestselling course. You must always stay open to new possibilities and think outside the box.

BECOME ACTIVE IN RELEVANT ONLINE GROUPS

Find various online groups (Facebook is a good place to start) where members of your target audience like to hang out. Start engaging with people, with your primary focus being on providing value. Don't try to sell anything. Don't even mention your course. For the first few weeks, focus purely on helping and connecting with others. If you start by building relationships, people will begin to wonder who you are and what you have to offer. In those cases, you can mention your course. However, stay humble and never openly sell in groups that don't allow it.

SAY YES! TO ALL SPEAKING ENGAGEMENTS AND RECORD THEM

I recommend that you book any speaking engagements that come your way, especially if you don't have much of an existing audience. At first glance you may think that presenting in front of 20 college students or members of a non-profit organization may seem like a waste of your time. However, with every presentation you'll gain valuable experience, hone your craft, and expose yourself to people who could potentially become your core supporters. You should always film your presentations, even if it's just with your phone, and ask someone to take some pictures. Then, use that content to build your portfolio and develop a stronger brand as a speaker. Showing stage shots on your course landing page will certainly add extra credibility.

Have you ever noticed how an introvert who's spent half of the conference sitting alone can suddenly become a micro-celebrity just by getting on stage? Before the talk that person may have been minding their own business sipping tea in the corner. Suddenly, after delivering a presentation, they're surrounded by a hungry mob asking questions and eager for more information.

This is known as the **stage effect**. It happens because we tend to associate being on a stage with status and authority. Whoever is selected to speak in front of an audience must be one of the most prominent experts, right? The answer is not always clear, but what matters is that this is the perception, and as we've noted, perception creates reality.

If you'd like to learn more tips about public speaking, you can find free resources on **www.jimmynaraine.com/coursecreation resources.**

DON'T OVERTHINK

I'd like to stress again that you don't have to do everything I'm outlining here. You could keep this as simple as posting a series of videos on social media, notifying your inner circle that you plan to launch a course, and then publishing on Udemy. Everyone reading this book has a different set of goals, priorities, and circumstances. That's why I'm giving you a wide array of options to consider.

THINGS TO REMEMBER

- Start building your email list immediately: Offer a high-value lead magnet enticing people to provide their email addresses.

- Regularly publish/repurpose content on various social media platforms to see what "sticks."

- Develop authentic relationships with podcasters focusing on providing value.

- Reach out to those who review online courses and offer incentives to them (e.g. affiliate commission) and their audience (e.g. steep discounts, free codes, bonuses).

- Instead of fiercely competing with other creators in your niche, focus on win-win collaboration opportunities.

- Build your credibility by sharing your expertise in various online groups. Eventually, people will ask you about your premium content.

- Accept and record all speaking engagements. Leverage the "stage effect" to boost your online credibility.

- Avoid paralysis by analysis. Choose the strategies and tactics you resonate with the most and get started.

CHAPTER 25

HOW TO DEAL WITH REVIEWS

YOUR REVIEWERS ARE GOLDEN

Treat your reviewers like members of your inner circle. When someone takes the time to watch your content and then post a formal rating, come on! You gotta appreciate that. Send a direct thank-you note to those people whenever you can. Initially, I used to do it all the time. Nowadays, with hundreds of weekly reviews, it's hard to stay on top of it. However, I still do my best to message as many people as possible because I know how much it means. Sometimes people respond to my thank-you note by writing something along the lines of: "Wow, thank you, Jimmy. I know you have many students, and it's awesome you took the time to reach out!" As you can imagine, this solidifies my relationship with those customers.

You may be wondering: "All of this makes sense, but what about bad reviews?" Getting negative ratings is always a touchy subject, especially for your ego. However, there's a smart way to deal with those situations.

First of all, always keep your ego in check. There is nothing worse than arguing with one of your customers; it can only damage your brand. The following ideas may prove very helpful at the beginning of your online journey, when every single review can impact your overall score.

Be brutally honest with yourself. Examine if the negative review you've just received may have some truth in it. If yes, save it and treat it as feedback that will help you to improve.

If the review is hateful, has swear words in it, or doesn't make any sense, make sure to notify the platform. In many cases, they remove such ratings.

If the review is negative, but not hateful, I recommend that you write a direct response. Here is the template you can use:

Hi <first name>,

First, thanks for taking the time to invest in this course, and I hope you found some value in it. I'm sorry to hear that you didn't totally enjoy it. Frankly, I do my absolute best to deliver as much value as possible to my audience, but I'm human, and sometimes my content doesn't resonate with everyone. I appreciate your feedback and would love to hear what I could add to the course to make it a five-star learning experience in your eyes.

All the best, and thanks again for being direct and transparent,

Jimmy

Sending something like this often disarms the other person. After all, it's expected that the negative review could make you furious. When you show someone respect despite their negative comment, it can sometimes shift their attitude. Moreover, expressing the willingness to accept brutally honest feedback suddenly makes you more likable. I've had instances where I've responded courteously to a bad review, and the person has changed their two-star review into a four-star or even five-star rating, apologized and admitted that they just had a bad day. Those situations never cease to fascinate me.

Here is how you can respond to a semi-positive review. You can use this template when you get a three or four-star rating:

> *Hi <first name>,*
>
> *First of all, thank you so much for sharing your feedback. I always do my best to give as much value as possible to my audience. I'm curious, is there anything I could do/ add to the course for you to feel like it's a five-star production? I always appreciate genuine feedback and do my best to implement suggestions. It would be great to hear from you.*
>
> *Have a great day,*
>
> *Jimmy*

You can't fully predict how people will react to such a response. However, based on my experience, many individuals will end up providing detailed feedback that's very useful for improving your content. Again, some of them go so far as to raise their initial rating. This is why respectfully responding to your reviewers can be so powerful. On the flip side, if you don't reply, there is zero probability you'll learn something useful or that your students will amend their ratings. They'll just move on, leaving you stuck with their negative comments.

THINGS TO REMEMBER

- Your reviewers are golden, so treat them as such. Expressing your genuine appreciation for their ratings fosters your relationship.

- Keep your ego in check after receiving negative reviews. Learn from constructive criticism, but report hateful comments.

- Responding respectfully to negative reviews sometimes propels people to amend them positively.

- Address impartial reviews by asking for specific suggestions.

CHAPTER 26

THINGS TO KEEP IN MIND WHEN RUNNING PROMOTIONS

EVERYONE WANTS TO GET THE BEST DEAL

There is an interesting psychological phenomenon called **the ultimatum game**. Two people are offered a certain amount of money by a stranger (let's say $1,000) and which can be split between them. However, only one of them can decide what the exact split will be. There are no rules, meaning the money could be divided evenly or the decision-maker could decide to keep most of it. The catch? If the other person is not satisfied with the amount they would get, he or she can cancel the deal, in which case nobody gets anything.

The fascinating thing is that people would rather not get anything than let another person keep the majority of the cash. Intellectually, this makes no sense. After all, any amount of free money is better than zero. However, experiments like this reveal something fascinating about human psychology. Namely, most people are very attached to the idea of things being "fair." Even though it goes against logic, most of us would rather not receive $100 if we know that the person who wasn't fair is rewarded with $900.

People love knowing that things are done fairly. Better yet, they love getting the best deals possible. That is why millions of Americans storm the shops during Black Friday sales. Even people who don't have stable finances end up buying into the frenzy of: "Woohoo! Let's grab the best discounts, so we don't miss out!"

How does this relate to selling online courses? When you run promotions in your classes, you need to make sure that the offer is so good that people can't refuse. They need to feel like your deal is not just fair, but ideally, irresistible.

SCARCITY

Scarcity occurs when something is in short supply and there is demand that can't be met. Creating the feeling of scarcity around your promotions assures that your customers don't procrastinate with their buying decisions. You can trigger a feeling of scarcity in various ways:

- Give a steep discount for a limited time, say 48 hours.
- Include free bonuses for a limited time.
- Limit how many people can take advantage of your offer (The first 30 customers receive a discount or some type of bonus, for example).

Remember, when running such a promotion you must always keep your word. Otherwise, you will quickly lose credibility. For instance, if you say your promotional coupons last for only 48 hours, make sure this is the case. If the discount is still active a week later, people will stop believing in your promotions.

Consequently, next time you run a sale, your existing customers might assume that the time limit is fake. This not only lowers your credibility but may also hurt your sales.

OFFER BONUSES

Who doesn't love a **bonus**? Suppose you want to buy some raspberries. Even though there may be several brands available, the moment you notice a massive "150 grams extra for FREE" label on the package, you are likely to grab it without double-checking what the actual price per gram is. It happens because we are hardwired to seek instant rewards, and this is what our brains perceive discounts and bonuses to be. A reward!

When running promotions, one of the best ways to make it a no-brainer is to offer gifts. This could be as simple as adding several fresh videos to your course or uploading PDF summaries for each lecture. You could also create separate audio files that people can download and listen to while on the go.

FREE PREVIEWS INCREASE CONVERSIONS

How comfortable are you buying something you can't see? This is how most course creators operate. They assume that people will purchase their products based solely on credibility factors and captivating trailers. However, nothing sells your content better than giving people a real glimpse into what they can expect after the purchase.

There's a reason why online course behemoths, such as Udemy, make **free preview** videos compulsory. After almost a decade of serving tens of millions of clients, they have concluded that such an approach is key. Even if you decide not to use Udemy as your platform of choice, make sure that you offer some type of free preview. Psychologically, doing so shows that you are confident in your content and have nothing to hide.

REGULAR UPDATES

Some marketers rely primarily on course launches to make money. They don't care if their classes have any longevity. I still remember promotions for those "get rich online" programs that would explicitly state: "This course will be deleted after the first week, so buy now." This extreme scarcity, combined with selling a dream of getting rich, would essentially force many individuals to buy on an impulse with the money they often couldn't afford to spend.

My approach is entirely different. I pride myself on building products that are designed to help people worldwide for years to come. To accomplish that goal, you must give your best to your viewers, and update your content periodically. Naturally, the extent to which you will perform **updates** will depend on various factors, but it's crucial that you don't launch a product and then simply forget about it.

MONEY-BACK GUARANTEE PAYS OFF

The first reaction I get from people when I outline the importance of the **money-back guarantee** is: "But how!? I can't afford for everyone to get their money back!"

Many content creators make the erroneous assumption that whenever given a chance, people will try to get their money back. This couldn't be further from the truth. In fact, in my ten years of selling courses to hundreds of thousands of people, my refund rate is consistently under 2%. Bear in mind that I host my courses on Udemy, where getting a refund is hassle-free and requires just a few clicks, yet my refund rate stays low.

How come more people don't want to get their money back? Contrary to what major news stations often lead us to believe, most people are inherently good by nature. From my experience, people appreciate the value you give them and are willing to pay for it. In fact, I noticed something fascinating. Over the years, I've even received messages that said: "I learned so much from your content. You should charge more."

When you allow someone to "test drive" your product without any risk, you develop immense trust. It also makes people feel much more comfortable about investing their money in your course. It gets them through the door, and if your content is valuable enough, most people will never look back.

Congratulations! You've now learned how to publish your course. You're also familiar with the essential elements of planning a successful launch and thriving marketing campaigns. Most importantly, you took the time to work through the entire process for how to create your first online course. You've proven that you have the dedication that any successful creator must have to be successful. Now let's move to the final section of this book.

THINGS TO REMEMBER

- Leverage psychological desire for fairness by offering unbeatable deals that customers can't refuse.

- Encourage prompt purchases with scarcity tactics, such as limited-time discounts, bonuses, or restricted availability.

- Enhance your promotions with attractive bonuses, making them irresistible to potential buyers.

- Boost conversion rates by offering free lecture previews, demonstrating confidence in your content.

- Ensure long-term value by regularly updating your courses.

- Build trust and incentivize purchases with a money-back guarantee, as most customers won't misuse the policy.

PART 6

HARNESS YOUR FEAR AND DEVELOP TRUE CONFIDENCE

Congratulations. You now understand what you need to do during the course creation journey and how the different pieces work together. As I'm sure you can see by now, something that initially felt overwhelming, maybe even insurmountable, turns out to be fairly straightforward.

In this part we'll discuss how to build your confidence to an undefeatable level. You may be tempted to skip this part, put this book back on the shelf, and jump right into the hands-on course creation activities. However, based on my experience with thousands of aspiring course authors, the number one reason preventing them from embarking on this journey is not external, but mental. Sadly, there are so many aspiring creators out there who, in spite of having complete clarity and a proven system at their fingertips, can't summon the courage to take the final leap. They've successfully completed 99% of the work, they've fought so many battles, but their inner demons are winning the war. Tragically, all their unique expertise remains unpublished. In this part of the book, let's focus on building the strong, internal foundation you need to take massive action and attain long-term success.

Have you ever done something so scary that your entire body was oozing in adrenaline? Perhaps it was a bungee jump, diving with sharks, riding your first big wave, interviewing for your dream job, or getting on a stage in front of a large audience? Maybe it was something seemingly simple, yet for some reason equally terrifying, like sharing bad news with someone, expressing your true feelings with a person you love, or admitting to a mistake you made? When faced with such a challenge, you have to make a choice. You either summon the courage and go for it in spite of the fear, or you give up before you even try.

Let me tell you about a fear I overcame and why it was so important to me to do so. For as long as I can remember, I wanted to experience what it feels like to jump out of a plane. Interestingly, however, every time an opportunity to take the leap presented itself, I would rationalize not going for it. Several years ago, I was exploring Hawaii, which is arguably one of the best places to sky-dive. One day I parked next to the skydiving center but couldn't get myself to leave the car. Instead, I sat safely inside, feeling the butterflies in my stomach gradually turning into anxiety. Eventually, I switched on the engine and drove off.

Sounds weird, right? My anticipation led to overthinking, which in turn triggered paralysis. I retreated back into my comfort zone.

Inside my head, I reasoned that since I'd already spent a lot of money on the car rental, I should make the most of it and explore the island instead. Looking back now that sounds cringeworthy to me, but back then it felt legitimate.

A similar episode took place in Australia just a few weeks later. No matter how much I tried, I couldn't summon enough courage to get on that skydiving plane. My head was full of excuses.

Finally, I went to Poland for Christmas. One morning I got out of bed with an unexpected "a-ha" moment—everything became clear in an instant. All the excuses I'd been crafting were really just a manifestation of a massive fear deep inside. A fear I needed to confront.

Have you ever had a sudden realization that changed the trajectory of your life? Well, this is what happened to me. Suddenly, I knew exactly what I needed to do. It wasn't just about skydiving. It was about me proving to myself that I was capable of facing my fears. So I did the only thing I could to make skydiving my only option. I switched off my rational mind and took the first irreversible step. I Googled "safest places to skydive."

Skydive Dubai popped up as the top recommendation (that's some enviable SEO right there). I checked their website, selected a jump date, paid in advance, and booked a trip to Dubai. My gut feeling told me this might not be enough to get me on that plane (or diving out of it), so I decided to do something scarier than the thought of the actual jump. I embraced public accountability. I began to tell everyone about my new challenge. I made a Facebook post sharing with all my friends that I was about to jump from a plane. There was no turning back now! After all, I'd put my money AND my word on the line.

Fast forward several weeks, and I found myself cramped in a small aircraft, flying 13,000 feet above Dubai. When the doors opened, the ice-cold air rushed into the cabin. I had been waiting for that moment for so many years. Suddenly, time stopped, and my heart pounded in my chest. I felt the sweat pouring down my back, the pumping pressure in my head, and a strange electric sensation on my skin. I'd entered the raw "fight or flight" mode.

"What the hell am I doing here?" I thought. When the go-light turned green, I was supposed to stand by the edge and throw myself out of a plane. Isn't it crazy? To throw yourself out of a perfectly functioning plane?

It's difficult to describe the emotions you experience in such a situation. It feels completely surreal, as if you are in a movie. When doubts began to emerge, I quickly reminded myself that it wasn't just about that jump. It was about proving to myself that I was capable of absolutely anything I put my mind to.

That skydive was a metaphor for life. We all have access to opportunities, but it requires courage to identify and fully embrace them. I exhaled. And I took the leap.

As soon as my feet left the plane, I dropped like a heavy stone, roughly 50 meters per second. Suddenly, all my anxiety, self-doubt, and fear were gone. Something else took their place. I felt exhilarated! Truly alive. Most importantly, though, I was in full control of my life. You see, most of our fears are just an illusion. We deprive them of their power by taking action. This was a perfect reminder, and I wanted that moment to last forever.

As you have read through this book, you may have heard your negative internal dialog kicking in: "Come on, you can't do it. It's too complicated, and it's too risky." The best way to crash this negativity is to *take little steps every single day* to counter your fears.

This book is an action manual. Don't merely read it. Follow the process; write things down as you study the blueprint. In fact, if you want to put extra pressure on yourself, share with your friends that you are committing yourself to creating a course. Putting yourself on the line with public accountability will make you more likely to take this journey seriously and truly commit. It could be as simple as making a social media post that says: "I'm reading *Course Creation Simplified,* and I'll be publishing my first online course in the next X months. Stay tuned." This will make it real.

In fact, feel free to tag me on Instagram (@jimmynaraine), and I will gladly reshare your post for extra accountability. To spice things up, if you share a picture holding my book, message me and I will have an exciting gift for you.

In this part, we will focus on overcoming your fears and building the confidence necessary to produce your first, beautiful online course. Even if you feel confident, I encourage you to at least skim this section, because you may stumble upon a golden nugget or thought experiment that will empower you further.

CHAPTER 27

CULTIVATING YOUR RELATIONSHIP WITH FEAR

Are you feeling insecure? That's fine. Everyone is insecure about something. Those frailties are precisely what makes you human. In fact, insecurities can help you make your work great. At any point, you may start experiencing a strange, yet familiar sensation in your stomach. You may begin to ponder:

- "What if people don't like my videos?"

- "What if I make a fool of myself?"

- "What if people reject me, and I end up getting horrible reviews?"

- "Am I qualified enough to teach?"

What if, what if, what if? As we already proved in Part 1 of this book, most of those "what ifs" are just limiting beliefs. I've seen way too many people who possess very valuable and transferable knowledge but who can't seem to launch a course because of irrational fear. What should you do in a situation like this?

Pause. Take a deep breath. Focus on your WHY. Realize you are creating those fears inside you.

Go ahead, create a course. Do your absolute best. However, put yourself at ease knowing that if you don't feel comfortable publishing your final product, you have no obligation to do so. If you feel overwhelming anxiety about posting a course online, alleviate that anxiety by treating the creation of your first course only as practice to become better. Don't get trapped in the downward spiral of overthinking; take the first constructive step to trigger positive momentum.

After reading this chapter, will you fully overcome all your fears? Nope. As long as you're a healthy human being you will keep experiencing certain doses of fear for the rest of your life. It's not only normal, but if properly channeled, that fear helps you to perform at your best. One of the most important keys to having success in any area of your life is not to avoid fear, but to dance with it.

Even the toughest people on the planet have to regularly embrace that dance. I'd like to share with you a powerful example that former Navy Seal and ultra-athlete David Goggins revealed during his Impact Theory video interview with Tom Bilyeu. At some point, he confessed that he was slightly trembling in his seat before the interview, and no, it wasn't the air conditioning. David went on to explain that some part of him was afraid that he would stutter. You see, he wasn't always the modern-day warrior he's now known to be.

From growing up with an abusive father, to enduring racist slurs and daily bullying, Goggins has transformed himself into a living legend. But that wasn't until after he'd experienced one of the lowest moments of his life. Desperate for a change, he quit his job spraying for cockroaches and set out to become a Navy Seal. Over the following months, he worked on himself like a maniac and lost almost 48 kilograms of weight in order to qualify for the grueling SEAL training. Due to major health challenges, he had to go through the infamous BUDS training three (!) times, but he wouldn't quit. Eventually, he entered the brotherhood, just as he'd set out to do.

However, that wasn't enough for Goggins. Once he learned that he could overcome fears and obstacles to reach high goals, he pushed himself mentally and physically to accomplish superhuman endeavors. Some of those feats have included breaking the world record for the most pull-ups in 24 hours and running 100+ mile races without stopping. Now, David inspires tens of millions of people around the world, including myself, and I highly recommend that you read his books: *Can't Hurt Me* and *Never Finished*.

Here is a question: How can one of the toughest people on the planet still experience self-doubt and fear? Knowing David's life story it's natural to assume that he has no insecurities. Why then was he trembling during the interview? The simple answer: He is a human being, and all healthy human beings feel anxiety, feel fear. But let's face it. Life without fear wouldn't be as fun; without challenges you would miss out on opportunities for growth. It's in the moments of bursting out of your comfort zone when you feel truly alive in the marrow of your bones.

THINGS TO REMEMBER

- Embrace insecurities as a vital part of the human experience. Use them to fuel your drive to create exceptional work.

- Confront limiting beliefs by focusing on your "why" and taking decisive action. To alleviate anxiety, perceive the launch of your first course primarily as a learning experience.

- Recognize that facing your fears and venturing beyond your comfort zone are catalysts for personal growth and a fulfilling life.

CHAPTER 28

DOUBLE YOUR CONFIDENCE

Let's focus on building unstoppable confidence. In this chapter, I'll share with you strategies and mindset shifts that will help you boost your confidence. I've used these tools during my workshops and private mastermind adventures to push people beyond what they ever believed was possible.

I've helped hundreds of people face their biggest internal demons by leading them to perform extreme activities—jumping from a 15-meter cliff into the ocean, spending several minutes in an ice bath, rope-jumping from a 160-meter bridge in Nepal, or climbing 150-meter steep cliff faces in Gran Canaria. I'm not sharing this to brag. I simply want to show you how powerful mindset shifts can be. You can do anything you put your mind to. All you have to do is learn to dance with the fear.

The good news is that pursuing extreme challenges is not the only way to overcome your limiting beliefs. You can work on many things internally and in the comfort of your home to boost your self-confidence.

SHAPE YOUR IDENTITY

Creating a powerful **identity** is one of the most important things you can do to build your confidence. First of all, what is identity? The *Cambridge Dictionary* defines it as: "Who a person is, or the qualities of a person or group that make them different from others." You can find a variety of definitions out there, but for our purposes, let's view it as: Who you perceive yourself to be at your core.

Unfortunately, most people have a weak or poorly defined identity. In fact, many people will admit they feel lost and don't even know who they are.

I still vividly remember when I was a teenager in post-communist Poland, trying to figure out what life was all about. I felt insecure, shy, and inadequate. My father had been born in Guyana and he'd come to Poland at the age of 18 to study medicine. Other kids always made sure to remind me that I was different. Through the years, I changed schools several times, always carrying the label of the "new kid." There was also a time in my life when I was mixed in with some shady characters. Back then, my identity was very fragile. I saw myself as a poor kid with the world scheming against me. I felt like I was inadequate, not socially savvy, and constantly misunderstood.

At some point, I discovered personal development and started consciously working on how I perceived myself. I became a ferocious learner, mastered English, and bootstrapped my way to a leading British business school. I began destroying my limiting beliefs as I came to realize that reality was just an illusion and I could bend it to my will. The narrative at my university was that entering the corporate world was the pinnacle of achievement. I succumbed to this belief and started working for Goldman Sachs in London. However, I soon realized that investment banking didn't give me any sense of purpose or feeling that I was contributing to the world. Eventually, I discovered my real mission. That's when I dove deep into entrepreneurship and the world of learning and education.

Shifting my identity was the catalyst for every milestone I have managed to attain since then. Now I understand what I didn't know back then. If you want to create any external change, first you need to shift what's happening inside your head.

What is your identity? What do you see and feel when you close your eyes and picture yourself? Is it negative or positive? No matter who you are, you can always work on making your identity sharper, stronger, more in focus. It's a never-ending journey. I keep working on it myself every day.

For example, my current identity is that *I'm a Spartan leader who is on a mission to help millions of people to overcome their limiting beliefs. I'm a protector willing to go through any pain to make a positive global impact. I'm an adventurer who lives life to the fullest.*

This powerful self-identity acts as fuel whenever I face challenges. For instance, writing this book was an exciting experience, but on some days, I didn't want to face the blank page. That's when my identity kicked in. After all, if I'm a leader who is willing to do whatever it takes to impact millions, how can I possibly give in to the temptation of slacking off? The moment I reminded myself of who I am, I felt the inner fire building up. It fuels me with energy and makes me want to attack my biggest goals.

What do you want your identity to be? Why not make "being a bestselling course author" a vital part of it? Perhaps you want to see yourself as a leader helping millions of people. Maybe you have children and want to be the best parent for them, but also a guiding light for kids around the world who don't have any mentors. Naturally, every single person is wired differently. Whatever your identity is, make sure it evokes emotion. Make sure that it drives you!

YOUR ACTION STEP

Take a piece of paper and "design" a new identity for yourself. Write it out. Make it compelling and vivid. For maximum impact, keep it under four sentences.

Your new identity will serve as your rock, source of inspiration, and a northern star guiding your actions. Read it out loud regularly. It's not merely about memorizing it. It's about embedding it in your brain and allowing it to shape the choices you make and who you become.

###

REAL-LIFE APPLICATION OF IDENTITY

I'll never forget the day I took some mastermind members on a cliff climbing expedition in the Canary Islands. At some point, the senior climbing instructor asked me to go through the next passage alone without my group. We climbed up a very steep cliff face I wasn't familiar with. As we got to the highest reachable point, I felt confused. After all, why would we choose this route if there was no direct way to reach the top? The answer shocked me. Juan casually handed me the end of a metal cable. The other end was hanging loosely from the very top (roughly 50 meters from us). I was supposed to clip myself in and swing to the other side of the cliff 50 meters above the ground.

My first thought was, "I'm not fucking doing this." However, once I regained my composure, a sudden realization filled me and strengthened me: "Why am I here? Why am I even doing this expedition in the first place if not to help my team overcome their limiting beliefs?"

I'd taken other people on the climb to show them that their fears were just an illusion, that they were capable of so much more than they realized. As a leader, my responsibility was to pave the way and fuel them with strength. Getting in touch with my identity was the spark I needed in that terrifying moment to transform from a fearful human being to a Spartan leader. I clipped myself in and swung swiftly to the other cliff. I then helped each team member to do the same.

If you want to publish a course, please, don't overlook this part of the process. Take some time now to create a powerful identity statement. It is fuel that will keep powering you. If you feel like sharing it, please do so on Instagram. If you tag **@jimmynaraine** I will definitely see it.

THINGS TO REMEMBER

- Boost your confidence by consciously working on your mindset, facing your fears, and smashing through what's holding you back.
- Create a compelling self-identity and deeply ingrain it.
- Ensure your new identity feels powerful, stirs positive emotions, and aligns with your dreams and values.

CHAPTER 29

CREATE SYSTEMS THAT MAKE FAILURE IMPOSSIBLE

While systematically working on your self-confidence is crucial, you also need a way to put your new-found confidence into action. Thus, it is essential that you create **smart systems** that will make it impossible for you to fail. The great thing about systems is that they keep you in check and on track. They also eliminate a lot of friction during decision making. If used properly, they force you to do what you should be doing whether you feel like it or not.

For example, let's imagine that you haven't really exercised during the past year. At the same time, you desperately want to get in shape. Your schedule is hectic, and the only time you could possibly carve out for your daily exercise is early morning. Unfortunately, you tend to be so sleepy after waking up that you need a shot of espresso just to kick-start your brain.

The question is: What would make you more likely to honor your commitment and go for a morning jog? Embark on a new challenge blindly or create a clever system?

If you rely solely on your willpower, here's how things are likely to look in the morning. You hit snooze on your alarm several times. Finally, you manage to get up, already irritated by the prospect of exercising. You prepare some coffee, and try to find your running gear. But then you realize that if you go for a jog now you may be late for work. You then rationalize that you no longer have a choice but to skip your morning jog. Later that evening, you feel bad about your behavior and feel an irresistible impulse to get a quick boost of "happy" hormones. You end up browsing social media late into the night. The next morning you feel even more tired and, once again, set aside your goal. You rationalize that you will most definitely start "tomorrow." As we both know, "tomorrow," "someday," and "one day," never come. Eventually, you start getting used to the idea of not getting in shape and you move on to other things.

Now, imagine that instead of relying solely on your willpower (and failing miserably), you implement a smart system to help you get out and jog in the morning. You set up a loud alarm that requires you to solve several math equations to turn it off (I personally use the Alarmy app). This way you have no choice but to wake up. You position your phone away from your bed, which forces you to not only wake up but to stand up. You program the coffee the night before so you can "down it" right after opening your eyes. Your running gear, a bottle of water, headphones, and anything else you may need are neatly positioned and ready to go. When you go to the bathroom you see hanging on the mirror a motivational quote, your fitness goal, and the picture of the physique you are training toward.

In this scenario, you aren't relying solely on your willpower and elusive motivation. The system you implemented removed friction from your decision making. Your environment no longer hurts you; it serves you. And you've eliminated potential obstacles before they can even emerge.

Despite some level of discomfort, you get fired up and go for a jog. Later that day, you have a sense of satisfaction that makes you sleep well at night. You repeat the process the next morning. The positive momentum builds up and you start noticing results. This fuels your inner drive, and eventually, your morning exercise becomes a powerful habit. Victory!

You may be wondering how smart systems could help you produce a successful course. Let's run through a powerful strategy that will keep you on your path in spite of fear, distractions, and difficulties.

ACCOUNTABILITY

Remember my skydiving story? I doubt I would have been able to take that leap without committing financially and letting all my friends know my plan. It's the power of public accountability that made my jump possible. People from all over the world use that same strategy to successfully publish all types of content. For example, several years ago my friend Renat Gabitov, together with a group of entrepreneurs, did a 30-day YouTube challenge. Their goal was simple—publish one video each day for 30 consecutive days. They succeeded thanks to the power of positive peer pressure.

Another friend, Martin Georgiev, who currently works at Google, used to run all types of accountability challenges during his entrepreneurial journey. For instance, he would often commit to a deadline by putting his money on the line. The premise was always the same. Martin would give 500 euros to one of his friends and state: "If I don't do what I'm supposed to do by the deadline, the money is yours." This may sound excessive to some people, but his results are unquestionable. Martin successfully used financial accountability to accomplish tremendous things, from creating online courses to quitting smoking.

Alternatively, you can create an accountability group on social media. Everybody in your team has to share their goals with other members, commit to following through, and post their daily/weekly/monthly progress. Being a member of such a group pushes you, since you know that you've committed to other people and they are waiting for your updates (as they share theirs). Not updating the group would project a lack of respect for the other members, as you've all made a strong commitment to one another. Therefore, you're more likely to take action because updating your team with poor results seems more painful than taking (often uncomfortable) action and doing what it takes to reach your goal. If you would like to join an accountability group follow my social media as I will be launching something exciting soon.

One great strategy I highly recommend is to find a partner who is on a similar path. Schedule a regular call where you discuss your objectives, progress, and self-doubts while also sharing techniques and strategies. Finding the right person may not be easy, but believe me, having an accountability partner can be a game changer. You will push each other to work harder and share important insights to elevate you both.

Here are several things you can do to embrace accountability when building an online course:

- Let people know that you are beginning the process. This in itself will spark positive pressure and make it real.
- Go further. Publicly commit to a specific publish date.

- Join or create an accountability group to push one another toward your goals.

- Use Martin's approach and embrace financial accountability.

- Register on the course platform(s) you plan to use with a free plan and explore the instructor dashboard. It's a powerful self-accountability move and will help you build "I'm a course author" identity.

THINGS TO REMEMBER

- Create intelligent systems that make failure less likely by reducing decision-making friction.

- Implement accountability measures such as financial commitments or public announcements to keep yourself on track.

- Use the power of positive peer pressure by joining or creating an accountability group.

- Find an accountability partner with similar goals. Share insights and strategies, and keep each other motivated.

PART 7

TAKING THE LEAP

Welcome to the final part of this book. What a ride it has been! I hope that by now you feel fully equipped to get your first course out there. Here, we'll recap what you have learned about course creation. I will also do my best to help you kindle and keep that fire in your belly alive.

In Part 1, we delved deep into your big "WHY" and examined all the reasons for building a course. You learned that it's not merely about creating an extra income stream and that becoming a course author will give you many other opportunities: You'll gain credibility as an expert and increase your global impact as your online courses set you on a path to becoming location independent; your courses will lead you to new clients for your business; and the valuable content you produce will contribute to your legacy.

The world is swiftly transitioning into an online, personal transformation economy. Today, creating and posting a solid course is something anyone can pursue. In fact, it's something you need to think about as soon as possible if you don't want to miss out on golden opportunities. If you act quickly, you can still capitalize on the fact that most of your competition is in perpetual procrastination mode. Yet, as people start shifting their mindset, the online marketplace will become more crowded. Now is an excellent time to establish yourself as an online thought leader in your category.

In Part 2, we put a lot of effort into planning your overall course strategy. You learned the importance of taking into account various factors to determine your direction: how to come up with your course topic by using online tools, researching the market, and implementing smart testing. You went through a comprehensive course positioning process, which is necessary to make sure that people find your course irresistible. And you defined your customer avatar, identifying their pain points and desires.

We also analyzed various strategies for building your class based on your primary objectives. And we discussed the importance of marketing funnels and why joining forces with your competition is not necessarily a bad thing. Most importantly, you received a menu of strategies you could successfully utilize based on your circumstances.

In Part 3, you learned the strategies for creating captivating content. I taught you everything you need to know about structuring your course from beginning to end to maximize its value for students. We also discussed how to distribute lectures across sections to increase engagement.

In that part of the book I also equipped you with all the necessary ingredients to create world-class content based on the things your customers care about most. On top of that, I taught you a step-by-step process for designing epic promotional video content that will dramatically increase your conversions.

In Part 4, we examined the various ways to get your course filmed. You learned how to overcome your fear of the camera as well as proven techniques for becoming a more compelling presenter. You also learned a very specific, step-by-step process to get your entire course filmed even on a minimal budget.

In Part 5, we talked about everything that has to do with publishing and marketing your courses. I showed you various strategies you could pursue and what online course platforms you could choose based on your objectives and current circumstances. I also shared a straightforward strategy for anyone who feels confused while building their first course without having any preexisting audience.

Moreover, we discussed well-tested marketing and branding strategies you could use to start building a loyal following from scratch. This included clever hacks and marketing tactics I used when creating my online course business.

Part 6 was all about building your confidence. You may think that your content isn't good enough and that nobody will buy your course. You may have a misconception that the course building process has to be lengthy and complicated. You may even believe that the camera doesn't like you and that you don't have what it takes to be on the world's virtual stage. Fortunately, we already demystified all of those fears to expose them for what they are: self-imposed limitations that have nothing to do with reality. Moreover, you've learned proven tools and strategies for building unstoppable confidence; and you've embarked on a powerful journey of self-empowerment so you can start perceiving yourself as a successful course creator. That new identity combined with clever systems implemented daily will make it impossible for you to fail.

Finally, we are here, almost at the finish line. My intention for this last chapter is to make the final push in terms of showing you that you are ready. You are ready to go out there and make your course a reality.

LOOKING BACK AND MOVING FORWARD

Something strange happened to me today. I was on a live video interview, and everything was going just fine. However, at some point, my friend asked me about my background. When I started telling her about growing up in post-communist Poland and my self-confidence and social anxiety issues, the unexpected happened. Suddenly I felt a surge of emotions that momentarily overwhelmed me. I needed to pause to regain my composure. I explained that if someone had told that young Polish kid back then that some of those big dreams would come true, he wouldn't have believed them. How could I have ever conceived the possible future of being able to travel around the world, helping hundreds of thousands of people? Especially when, as a boy, I didn't speak English, and I had no money, no connections, and no belief in myself?

I don't know you personally, but I know there are things you've managed to create in your life that felt impossible to accomplish in the past. You must give yourself some credit. You may face fears and self-doubts, but ultimately you are the one in control of your life.

Think about various milestones you've accomplished in your life. I bet some of those at some point seemed almost impossible. Remember your first day at school or university, looking at the list of required reading? Perhaps, your initial thought was: "There's no way I can go through all of those books!" However, when you focused on one book and one page at a time, it became possible. Maybe even enjoyable!

Perhaps you still remember the shock and exhilaration you felt when landing that dream job? Or when you finally had a conversation in a foreign language even though you were convinced it would never happen? Look at your partner. Do you remember the first time you felt something for that person, wondering if it would ever work?

I could share plenty of examples, but the bottom line is this: No matter who you are, you have already accomplished things that once seemed impossible. You are better than you think you are and you need to remind yourself of it. Building your first course is no different. I know the journey ahead may feel overwhelming. Isn't that true of anything else you've ever pursued in your life?

You get to decide what you will focus on today. Each one of those decisions will determine your future reality.

Is course creation easy? No.

Is it simple? Yes, as long as you follow the process and avoid toxic perfectionism and overthinking.

Instead of pondering all the limitations you think you may have, imagine instead your future self. Twelve months from now you're looking back, knowing that you were holding a course creation recipe in your hands. How would it feel to know that you didn't take action even though you were given all the necessary guidance and tools to move forward?

On the other hand, imagine that you are looking back, thinking: "Wow, this was one hell of a journey! I can't believe how much I've pushed myself! One year ago, I read Jimmy's book, and now I'm a legitimate course author." Imagine going to your course dashboard and seeing hundreds of top reviews from people who were positively impacted by your videos. Envision how that would make you feel.

Our world is shifting dramatically. What used to feel like science fiction ten years ago is becoming our new reality. I may be wrong, but I believe that the COVID-19 crisis has triggered something that cannot be undone. People are starting to truly appreciate online education. They value its simplicity, universal access, low cost, and personalization. Also, an increasing number of people are now perceiving peer-to-peer learning as being just as valuable as obtaining credits from top academic institutions.

As an expert in your field, you have a decision to make. You can approach your business through the lens of the old (and being abandoned) ways of the world, or you can adapt. Based on what has been happening over the past several years, the trajectory seems predictable. More and more people are moving into online space to get their education. Simultaneously, universities and other educational institutions have learned to adapt and offer online curricula. Today is the perfect time to start building your online education business.

Whether you want it or not, you already have an online brand. If you don't have anything published, your brand simply says: "This person doesn't have any content" to anyone searching your name. If you don't create a course, you are not just staying in the same place. You are actually lagging behind as other people, including your competitors, establish their online presence. If you want to thrive in this shifting economy, you need to start building a solid foundation. It won't happen overnight, of course, so you may as well get started right away.

SET A DEADLINE

Setting a deadline is extremely important. Financial writer Gail Vaz-Oxlade famously said that "a goal without a deadline is just a dream." You have your entire game plan now. In this book you've learned everything you need to know in order to birth your online course. Now is the time to truly commit by setting a deadline and embracing the power of accountability. Pick a date that is exciting, but also realistic, then tell everyone about it. In essence, by closing off your escape route you will maximize the probability of accomplishing your goal. Sure, you may experience roadblocks and self-doubts. We all do. However, when you set a firm deadline and keep reminding yourself of your big WHY (Part 1), you will keep the fire alive and become a published course author in no time.

DAILY HABITS

William Faulkner famously said: "I only write when I am inspired. Fortunately, I am inspired at 9 o'clock every morning."

I resonate with this a lot. My motto as a course creator is: "Don't wait for inspiration.Trigger inspiration."

Don't fall into the trap of waiting for the perfect moment to create content. This is as futile as asking your leg muscles to get stronger so you can run faster. By setting a daily habit of consciously working to bring your course to life, you become much better at triggering inspiration at will.

Here are tools you can use to build helpful daily habits:

- Use distraction blocking software to improve your focus. Various applications can block social media for specific amounts of time so you can concentrate on work. My absolute favorite is an app called **Cold Turkey Writer** that blocks your entire laptop until you finish typing a specific number of words. The only thing you see is a white screen and the progress bar.

- Set up regular reminders to keep your eyes on the mission. For example, several times a day, I receive notifications on my phone (I set up using a regular alarm app) with questions that nudge me toward my goal. *Are you focusing on your craft or wasting your time?Are you getting important things done or just squandering your opportunities?* Whenever I slack, one such reminder can get me back into my balance.

TRACK YOUR PROGRESS

It's crucial that you spend at least five minutes a day to measure your progress and adjust your direction along the way. This awareness will keep you moving forward and provide a constant surge of motivation as you aim for course publication.

KEEP FUELING YOUR MOTIVATION

Finally, no matter how driven you are, consciously work on keeping the fire alive by reading books, watching inspiring speeches, repeating affirmations, and reminding yourself of your vision. Do whatever works for you and be willing to experiment.

In his online masterclass, Dan Brown shared that when he was writing one of his books he printed a mock cover of the title he was working on and pasted it onto an existing book. He began each day by holding the book in his hands. He would feel its weight and texture, constantly reminding himself that his new book already existed in his mind, and he just needed to get those words out on paper.

This genius approach takes the power of **positive visualization** to the next level. Whatever path you embrace, make sure you keep your motivation alive.

A FEW FINAL THOUGHTS

I would like to leave you with a short yet powerful story about doing what's right despite fear and self-doubt. Laird Hamilton is one of the greatest big wave surfers in history. One day when the ocean was particularly fierce, Laird tried to surf waves the size of a building. In order to ride waves this big, you need someone on a jet ski to pull you out into the right starting position. Laird grabbed the end of the rope, and his partner accelerated to get him in the perfect take-off spot. Unfortunately, an unpredictable, monstrous wave bore down on them and they both ended up getting "wiped out."

In the surfing world, a *wipe out* means getting pummeled, like a ragdoll, by a wave. It can be a pretty scary experience, because you need to fight against your natural instinct to get to the surface as quickly as possible. The tricky thing is, you can't ever win against the force of the wave. As you are getting smashed down by the water, you have to stay calm, control your emotions, and patiently wait for the wave's grip to become weaker. That's when you make your way to the surface to catch a breath.

I'm an avid surfer, and I know this feeling too well. I have gotten wiped out by three-meter-high waves; the experience is terrifying. When you are being thrown around without the ability to breathe and you are completely losing your sense of up and down, even five seconds feels like an eternity. Imagine what it's like to get hit by a 15-meter wall of water, like Laird. And then, just as you are about to reach the surface, desperately trying to catch a breath, another one bulldozers over you.

Laird and his friend were unlucky that day. Laird was in one piece, but his friend got crushed on a reef, was badly injured, lost consciousness, and was bleeding profusely. Laird knew that if he didn't act quickly his friend's death was imminent. He dug deep into his energy reserves, managed to carry his friend out of the water, and then let the emergency medics take over from there. His partner was in terrible shape but at least his life was no longer in danger.

What happened next seems insane, even reckless by most peoples' standards. However, to me, it is a perfect illustration of the warrior spirit. I think that even as content creators, we can learn a lot from it.

After Laird's friend was safely transported to the hospital, Laird got back into the ocean and surfed several more gigantic waves. Let's pause for a moment. When most individuals hear this story, the immediate reaction is, "This guy is insane! He must be fearless!"

The thing is, Laird's amygdala, the part of the brain that triggers fear, was working just fine. In fact, according to what he said in an interview, he was scared shitless when he went back into the ocean. However, deep inside, he knew that if he didn't go back into the water right away the fear would have enough time to build up to the point of total paralysis. If he let that happen, he knew that he would never surf again.

Why is that?

Well, the interesting thing about fear is that it becomes increasingly overwhelming whenever you stop taking action. You may experience a tiny bit of fear today, but if you don't do anything about it, soon it may induce total paralysis. Laird understood this and knew that going back into the ocean was his only chance to continue his journey as a big wave surfer.

I'm sure that you've heard the old saying: "Get back on the horse," and I believe there is a lot of truth in that saying. If you get "bucked off" on your course creation journey, you need to get back on right away. One of the best ways to maintain control over your fears is to build momentum and do everything in your power to keep it. The good news is that reading this far into the book is proof that you already have tremendous momentum. You've gone through every single detailed step you need to know to publish a fantastic course. Now it's up to you to keep that positive spiral going, to keep that fire in your belly alive.

You need to know one more thing. Even though I've released more than 30 courses, I get butterflies every time I click that "publish" button on a new product. I still face self-doubts. Those feelings are normal. All those strong emotions only show us how much we really care. Just make sure that you don't allow them to stop you. It may be easy to rationalize that you're not ready, that you should shoot extra videos, or rethink your strategy. In most cases, it is just procrastination disguised as logical thinking.

After reading this book, you've got your roadmap. You know what to do to make your dreams a reality. So go ahead, keep riding that wave, and if you wipe out… catch another one. It will be so exciting to receive a message from you soon that says: "I did it, Jimmy! I'm a published course author now, and my content is helping people!"

Nothing would mean more to me. My mission is to help you and thousands of people like you overcome your limiting beliefs. I truly believe in the ripple effect. Together we really can have a positive global impact.

If you've found this book helpful, I would love to hear your thoughts. Honest reviews on platforms like Amazon help people to find exactly what they need, and I appreciate you sharing your feedback. Feel free to tag me on social media (**@jimmynaraine**) whenever you reach your career milestones. Hearing that my readers are doing well always warms my heart!

Thank you for taking this journey with me! Investing your valuable time with me means a lot. Finishing this book is living proof that you have a course in you. You just have to let it out. Remember that there are no limits to what you can do. Be bold. Share your unique expertise with the world. You may not fully know it yet, but your audience is waiting for you and depends on you.

- **Jimmy**

Made in United States
Orlando, FL
15 July 2024

49007239R00153